AN EVENING TELEGRAPH ARCHIVE PUBLICATION

MEMORY LANE
Scunthorpe & District

By Chris Horan & Nigel Fisher | **A century of life in northern Lincolnshire**

AN EVENING TELEGRAPH ARCHIVE PUBLICATION

MEMORY LANE
Scunthorpe & District

By Chris Horan & Nigel Fisher | A century of life in northern Lincolnshire

Breedon Books
Publishing Company
Derby

First published in Great Britain by
The Breedon Books Publishing Company Limited
Breedon House, 44 Friar Gate, Derby, DE1 1DA.
1999

ISBN 1 85983 176 1

Printed and bound by Butler & Tanner Ltd., Selwood Printing Works,
Caxton Road, Frome, Somerset.

Colour separations by GreenShires Ltd, Leicester.

Jackets printed by Lawrence-Allen, Avon.

Contents

Foreword

AS we approach the new Millennium it is worth reflecting on the rich seam of history which Scunthorpe and northern Lincolnshire has rendered over the past century.

We know from readers' letters, and telephone calls to our office, that 'Nostalgia' is one of the most popular features in the *Scunthorpe Evening Telegraph*.

People just love to look back on how things used to be.

Our weekly 'Nostalgia' column, and special 'Nostalgia' publications, are read avidly with copies being sent around the world to former Scunthorpe area residents.

With the new Millennium approaching it is an ideal time to produce a hard-backed book looking back over decades of unprecedented change in the history of the Scunthorpe district.

Your *Evening Telegraph* has reported on triumphs and tragedies, civil and industrial disasters, royal visits, sporting achievements and the lesser events that did not make banner headlines, but which were not, nevertheless, too small for us to record.

We need to acknowledge the work of our staff photographers down the decades who have supplied so many superb illustrations to the ever-growing *Telegraph* archive around which this book is based.

But the *Telegraph* would be nowhere without its readers.

And scores of photographs of everyday events,

people and places have been submitted to us by willing members of the public who know that their treasured snaps will interest so many other nostalgia-lovers.

To each and every one of them we send our sincere thanks.

Peter Moore,
Editor,
Evening Telegraph

Introduction

WITH the Millennium very much in mind, we take our readers on a voyage down Memory Lane, capturing the flavour of the varying decades of the 20th century.

And what better way to view the past 100 years than through the cameras of local photographers and the words of local people?

They make a tremendous double act and have brought to life and captured the mood of some of the extraordinary events of those changing times.

We hope that you enjoy this book just as much as we have putting it together and will continue to dip into its contents, again and again, breezing through the scenes of the century.

It has been a very difficult task indeed to sift through thousands upon thousands of pictures, all of which could stake a valid claim for inclusion.

But we have taken great care to include as wide a cross-section as we can, in an attempt to cater for everyone from the sporting fan to the pub-goer and the railway buff to the son of the soil.

Chris Horan and Nigel Fisher

People and Places

The balloon of Signor Alfonso Vonwiller and Lieut Cianetti of the Italian Army that descended on a house in New Holland on October 1, 1906, during an international balloon race which had begun in the Tuileries Gardens, Paris, the previous day.

Barnetby Silver Band *c*.1919. Left to right: Hubert White, Jack Braithwaite, Wilfred Denton, Reginald Gammidge, William Percival, Herbert Gammidge, George Rowntree, Thomas Cook, Amos Unknown, Herbert Gammidge Snr, William Hawksworth, Harold Howard, Dudley White, Alfred Gammidge, George Baker, David Baker.

This must be one of the earliest scouting photographs taken in North Lincolnshire. It is of the Brigg troop around 1910 – only a few years after the formation of the movement by Baden Powell.

Scouts from Brigg enjoying their Twigmoor Weekend in July, 1964 with grammar school masters Geoff Jarvis and Jack Moore (back row).

People today often get cynical about political matters and local government but there is no doubting the excitement that was caused in Scunthorpe in 1936 by the setting up of the borough council – a real sign that the town had arrived in economic terms. These residents sum up the feeling of the town with talk of success and prosperity, the Great Depression still being fresh in the memory. The Charter of Incorporation as a borough was handed over by the Rt Hon The Earl of Derby at a ceremony at the Old Showground on October 10, 1936 coming into effect on November 9. The formation of the borough united the villages of Ashby, Brumby, Crosby, Frodingham and Scunthorpe.

Co-op milk girls looking very smart indeed in the 1930s. The young lady seated on the right of the photo was Nancy Quartley. The girls delivered milk with horse and carts.

Scunthorpe Strength and Fitness Club members in the 1930s. Back, left to right: Connie Bielstein, Edna Payne, Ena Cross. Front: Dorothy Payne, Violet Franklyn. The ladies' section of the club used to meet in premises off Oswald Road and practise routines on the Old Showground in Doncaster Road.

This picture was taken during World War Two and would go nicely with the catchphrase of the Sergeant Major in *It Ain't Half Hot Mum* – 'Fine pair of shoulders, show 'em off!' Actually it's the Brumby senior boys school vaulting club display team of 1941-42 – a very fit looking bunch of lads.

Garthorpe Rose Queen celebrations in the 1950s. The event was organised by the Village Hall committee. The village hall at that time was the old Primitive Chapel in Shore Road. The site is now occupied by Garthorpe Village Hall.

The circus came to Ashby around 1955 and was on a field off Burringham Road, close to where the Beacon Hotel is today. This view is of the elephants parading down Ashby High Street. The houses featured are now shops and include Foster's fruitiers, Madoc Books and Cope's confectioners.

When Billy Smart brought his famous circus to Scunthorpe in the early 1960s, *Circus Boy* – starring Micky Dolenz of Monkees fame – was one of the best-loved TV programmes for local children like these, seen at Britannia Corner.

Canon Chappell, well-known vicar of Brigg, greets members of the Brigg Urban District Council as they arrive at St John's Church. He is shaking hands with Ernie Taylor, who ran a TV/radio repair and toy shop in Wrawby Street where the local lads went to buy their Dinky Toys. Centre, with the glasses, is J.J.Magrath, clerk to the UDC and later Brigg Town Council. In the background is Layne's garage.

Personal Memories

Fred Gilleard recalls the great days of village dances

PRIMITIVE conditions in a rural community are recalled by Fred Gilleard of Fockerby who remembers digging holes in the back garden to dispose of domestic night soil.

Fred (74) has always lived in Station Road, Fockerby, and is a witness to dramatic changes in agriculture and village life.

His home overlooks the course of the old River Don which divided the Archbishoprics of York and Canterbury and also served as the border between the former West Riding of Yorkshire and the Lindsey area of Lincolnshire.

It was the meandering Don which helped furnish the northern Isle of Axholme and Marshlands with rich alluvial deposits. Its diversion and drainage of surrounding land by the Dutchman Vermuyden patterned today's agrarian landscape.

Nowadays Fockerby and Garthorpe on the Lincolnshire side of the divide run into one. Fred can remember the river bed in Station Road being a deep ditch in the 1930s. It is now occupied by houses. A section down Ness Lane and Island Lane has also been filled in, though even today signs denoting both villages stand side by side.

Fred attended Garthorpe School and Crowle School, starting work aged 14 as a bricklayer for Kelsey and Sons of North Street, Crowle. Like many in those days he had also laboured on the land, leading a horse with an implement for breaking up the soil prior to potato harvesting and picking peas in the pod.

He served in the Navy during the war and later had a building and carpentry business with his brother Joseph.

"In the olden days everyone who lived here worked on a farm. Farms that employed 20 now run on one or two. It is the machinery that did it."

His father, Tom, who owned a Morris 8, one of the first cars in the village, was an exception to the rule, working as a first hand at Lysaght's Normanby Park Steelworks, Scunthorpe. Fred remembers other villagers calling to ask if he could get them a job.

"I can remember them putting piped water in about 1935." Before then the family had a well with water pump outside the back door.

"I remember electricity coming in; before then we had paraffin lamps."

Today the twin villages boast a Post Office with limited shop facilities but in his childhood there were a number of shops including Wardle's, Fillingham's, Buttrick's and Lockwood's. Grocery lorries from the Co-op and butcher carts from Luddington and

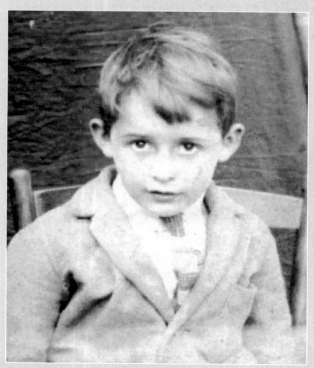

Fred Gilleard of Station Road, Fockerby, aged six.

Station Road, Fockerby around 1910.

Swinefleet also visited the community. At the time of writing, the Bay Horse, the only remaining pub, had been closed some months. Fred recalled earlier this century there was the Plough Inn on the corner of Island Road and Cross Street, plus Webb's Hotel by the ferry across the Trent to Burton Stather.

The opening of Keady Bridge in 1916 saw trade on the ferry decline and with it the demand for the hotel. It ceased in the 1930s. The ferry area was out of bounds during World War Two when amphibious craft were tested on the Trent.

Fockerby railway station closed for passenger traffic around 1933 but the sugar beet harvest and other freight was still taken out by rail into the 1950s. Bus links remain to Goole and Scunthorpe but their frequency is much reduced.

"There used to be dances here every fortnight in the Village Hall and we had a football team and cricket team. I have seen three bus-loads go to cricket matches from here," said Fred who lamented the passing of the dances and sporting teams.

Fred Gilleard is on the extreme left of this group, visiting Cleethorpes around 1937 with younger brother George, mother Sybil and a relative, Mrs Gilleard.

Tansy the Tramp was a very colourful character indeed in Brigg and was always to be seen in the town centre with one of his collection of battered prams. If teased by local children he would see them off with an angry wave of his hefty stick. He lived in an old outbuilding at Sumpter's Farm, Cadney Road. This picture dates from the late 1960s.

'You'll like it – not a lot'. Top TV magician Paul Daniels entertaining young fans during a visit to Scunthorpe.

Star of one of television's longest running and most popular series, *Doctor Who*, actor Tom Baker proved to be as entertaining off the screen as he is on it during a visit to the *Scunthorpe Evening Telegraph's* offices. He's seen here with some of the staff but is using a rather more conventional means of communication than the Tardis.

Carolyn Jones was a big star in the hit TV series *Crossroads* when she was invited to Scunthorpe's Family Weekend in June, 1979.

Personal Memories

Ron Shipley remembers "When I was a Lad..."

ON A DULL October morning in 1955, a 15-year-old boy cycled over the hills from Westwoodside to Epworth, to start his first day's work for Barnes and Breeze, publishers of the *Epworth Bells and Crowle Advertiser*.

There was no chance of him knowing that, 34 years later, he would be in the town again to start a new newspaper, the *Axholme Herald* and become its first and current editor.

The youngster was Ron Shipley, who joined the old printing firm as an apprentice compositor.

"Things were different in those days. I had to serve a six-year apprenticeship that continued until almost a year after my marriage," he said. "When I married, the wage was £9 10s, but after that first week in 1955, I received £1 16s 7d."

Since those days, most things have changed dramatically. Newspaper technology is light-years ahead of when Ron first set type by hand from a dusty case.

Ronald Shipley, aged 11 years.

He has lived all his life in Westwoodside. It was primarily a rural village, with leafy lanes, fields surrounded by tall hawthorn hedges, frogs and sticklebacks in the dykes – and hardly a pesticide in sight!

Wild flowers and plants grew at the roadside and a great variety of birds were in evidence, some of which are now being listed as endangered species.

Ron's earliest memory was of watching a wartime 'doodlebug' crossing the night sky. As it passed over the village, a bright flame appeared from this flying bomb, which later crashed and exploded in a field on the outskirts of Epworth.

Ron comes from a Methodist family, attending the village Sunday School from being two years old and also the evening chapel service.

The big Sunday School event was the anniversary in mid-May. Most children dressed in new clothes for these special events.

For the anniversary, they sang special hymns and the youngsters would either sing or say a poem. An anniversary tea and another service would follow on the Monday evening.

Although a Methodist, Ron attended the Church of England schools at Westwoodside and Haxey. The school buildings were Victorian and little had changed in the succeeding 40 years. There was no canteen and only a cold water tap existed in the cloakroom.

Each teacher managed two classes, but there were only a dozen or so pupils in a class. Everyone sat at their own desk in rows facing the teacher. Great attention was paid to learning the three 'Rs' – reading, writing and (a)'rithmetic.

It was important that everyone should learn their times tables from two to 12 and these were chanted daily. There was also a daily dose of mental arithmetic and if anyone got less

Booth's garage on Doncaster Road, Westwoodside, now Saab's garage.

The Carpenter Arms, Westwoodside.

Ron Shipley in the *Herald* office.

A shop in Ramper Road, Westwoodside.

than five out of ten at Haxey School, they received a crack across the fingers with a wooden rule – the cane for more serious offences.

Village life has changed greatly in Westwoodside. Housing estates now stand, where there were once fields, which gave a living to many a small farmer and his family.

Now, only a small fraction of the farming population exists, compared with 50 years ago.

It was a time when farmyards were occupied by bullocks, pigs, cows and horses. Hundreds of gallons of milk were collected daily by Northern Dairies for bottling.

Only the more affluent farmers had tractors – the horse was still used for most jobs by the other smallholders. Ron's father was forever a horseman, never taking a liking to tractors.

"Soon after the horse had passed from village life, so did some of the joy we got from our coveted country lifestyles."

Books like this one owe a huge debt of thanks to photographers down the ages who have recorded events for posterity. Harry Singleton, for many years the most prominent photographer in Scunthorpe, had a wooden hut he called a studio on land opposite the Oswald Hotel in High Street.

Ivor Anderton on the Alkborough Hill Climb. The River Humber is in the background. Photo *c*.1950.

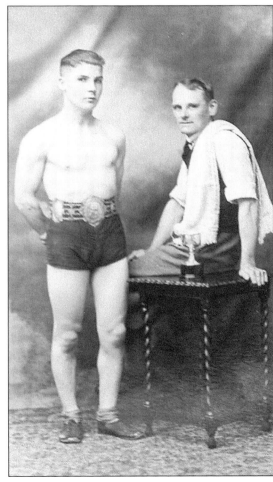

Althorpe trainer Fred King with champion boxer Harry Jenkins of Gunness. Fred trained boxers in a gym at the Dolphin Pub on the banks of the River Trent before the pub moved with the building of the A18 bypass road.

Undoubtedly one of Scunthorpe's greatest achievements on the zany side of life was achieved with the making of the World's Biggest Sausage in 1966. It was a team effort by 30 master butchers and their staff who assembled the sausage in the Rowland Road Co-op warehouse on June 29, 1966. The longest sausage measured 3,010ft long and weighed 8.5 hundredweight. Scunthorpe's record as world sausage beaters stood unchallenged for almost 10 years until April 18, 1976 when it was finally outrun.

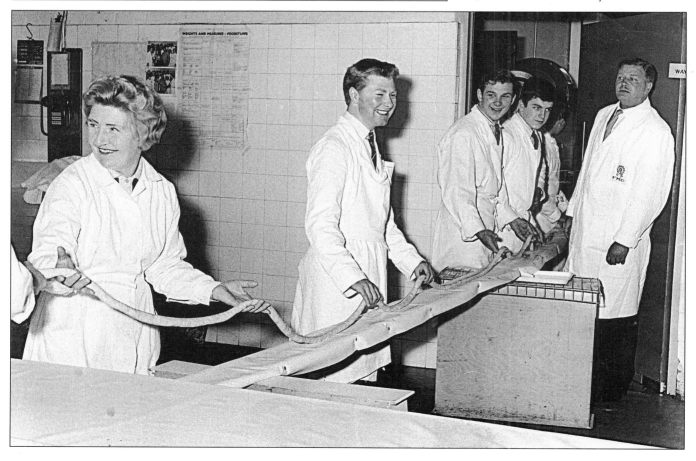

Scunthorpe butcher David Jenkins and branch manager Tony Walters with reputedly the world's longest giant lamb roll in 1972 which had been made from 61 breasts of best English lamb, stuffed and trussed with 250 strings.

Farmer Bob Trewick removes a Maltese Cross from the ruins of Temple Bellwood, near Belton, during the early 1970s.

Horticultural shows have long been a popular feature of rural life in the Scunthorpe area, with months being spent nurturing prize produce to the peak of perfection. Here the marrows are being measured at the Broughton Ex-Service Horticultural Show of 1979.

Personal Memories

Bramwell Millest recalls life with the Salvation Army

A NEAR century of change in Scunthorpe has been witnessed by Salvation Army member Bramwell Millest of Yaddlethorpe.

Bramwell Millest in his Scunthorpe fire brigade uniform c.1940.

He was born at 11 Mary Street, Scunthorpe, where he lived until marrying his wife Lily aged 24, whence they moved to Alexandra Road, Ashby.

Bramwell has seen the town grow from a collection of villages divided by green fields to an urban sprawl with streets renamed as the communities coalesced.

He attended Clayfield Road School which was still standing in the street known today as Doncaster Road until 1998 when it made way for a supermarket.

In those days everyone had a bicycle and the Scunthorpe and Frodingham Urban District Council operated with horses and carts and the odd steam roller.

His first work was casual pea picking but like his father Henry, he was also a fireman and among the blazes he attended was a spectacular one at Bradley's scrapyard on June 5, 1939, his birthday.

His main job after school was operating a greengrocer's round with horse and dray for Slater Espin of Ashby who had premises in Chapel Street, later renamed School Lane. His wage was five shillings a week.

Bramwell recalled walking to work from Scunthorpe on a rural pathway which came out

Bramwell Millest and his fruit cart on Ashby Road between Brumby Corner and Lincoln Gardens in the 1930s.

Bramwell Millest attended Bradley's scrapyard fire on Normanby Road, Scunthorpe, on June 5, 1939, his 22nd birthday. It was one of the biggest fires in town for some years.

The Millest family of 11 Mary Street, Scunthorpe, around 1935. Back: Roland, Hilda, Bramwell, Gordon, Eva, William. Front: Norman, Esther (mother née Ball), Daniel, Henry (father), Kathleen.

in Ashby, close to Collum Avenue. His passage was subject to diversions in 1933 when the Kingsway/Queensway Scunthorpe bypass Road was being built.

He said the road, like Ashby Road (which he calls Ashby Top Road), had been a single carriageway. He recalled it relieved congestion down Scunthorpe High Street which was a notorious bottleneck in the stretch between Woolworth and today's market hall.

After the war he was initially employed at Scunthorpe Borough Council gas works in Dawes Lane (the gasworks had previously been in Doncaster Road) but he then joined the Highways Department and subsequently the Health and Cleansing Department.

Bramwell remembers driving the first mechanical sweeper in Scunthorpe around 1948 and that the early dust freighters (dustcarts) had controls like those in trams and

a maximum speed of 26 miles an hour.

He has been bandmaster of the Scunthorpe Salvation Army in Cole Street and Ashby Salvation Army which had premises in Ashby High Street, Modder Street, Ashby, and Collum Lane, Ashby. What were separate units are now one.

Bramwell, who has played the cornet into his 80s, became a senior bandsman in 1934. He recalls the Salvation Army running soup kitchens in the 1926 strike and in 1929. He also remembers the Army preaching to drinkers leaving the old Oswald Hotel and the Blue Bell in Scunthorpe High Street. The former is now the Tavern and the latter was demolished in the late 1960s.

Up to the 1950s many homes in town were heated by coal fires prior to smokeless zones, but Bramwell said that, with few cars, in his opinion the atmosphere was cleaner than today.

Markets

The past century has seen a decline in the number and range of North Lincolnshire markets as shopping and agricultural patterns have changed. This typical scene records a proud moment for Harold Richards whose stall on Scunthorpe Market was voted the best of them all in terms of layout. He won a set of cutlery. However, Mr Richards had to close his stall and shop at 175 Frodingham Road when World War Two broke out, because of the difficulty of getting regular supplies. He then went into the steelworks.

Scunthorpe market drawing the crowds some 30 years ago. Note the children's roundabout, which was offering rides at six old pence.

A typically busy scene inside Scunthorpe market with shoppers eagerly seeking out a bargain.

A view from above showing a good selection of market stalls in Scunthorpe. This is looking towards Market Hill, prior to the building of the Binns store (Upton's) which was under construction in 1975.

The wheel has turned full circle in Brigg. As this picture from the turn of the century shows, shoppers used to be able to wander about between the market day stalls without the internal combustion engine getting in their way. When cars and lorries came onto the scene, Brigg town centre was transformed. But, in recent years, an ambitious pedestrianisation scheme has removed the through traffic and allowed shoppers and traders to go about their business in peace.

A scene gone forever – beasts being auctioned at Brigg cattle market. Dwindling trade was the cause of the closure, and the stockmarket – the pride of Brigg Urban District Council in the 1960s – has now been demolished to be replaced by the new Tesco superstore.

A lorry from Pinnock Farms of Barton at Brigg cattle market in the early 1970s. There were also cattle markets in Scunthorpe, Barton and Barnetby in the past.

Brigg cattle market in 1972 when it was still doing a good trade.

Although often called Brigg cattle market, the Cary Lane site also saw its fair share of sheep.

Stennett's market has long been a feature of Thursdays in Brigg, with buyers able to bid at auction for anything from an old lawnmower to a plump bird for Sunday dinner. Housed for a long time in Manley Gardens it moved over to the old stockmarket site in Cary Lane for a time before being relocated to Station Road.

Shops

The Co-op in Crowle. Those pictured include (from the left) Ralf Waterland, Billy Shepard, Fred Chafer, Mr Bellamy, Frank Parkin. Mr Bellamy was the manager. The opening of the new bridge at Keadby made it possible for the Scunthorpe Society to deliver goods on the west side of the River Trent and so, in order to avoid overlapping, amicable arrangements were made with the Goole Co-operative Society to take over the business of their Crowle Branch from January 1, 1917.

Kirman's hardware store in Market Hill on the corner of Chapel Street, Scunthorpe. The business was founded by Herbert Kirman in 1904 who bought the premises of J.W.Gunn. Most folk from the older generations in Scunthorpe will recall the name Kirman and have memories of the hardware stores in Market Hill, Chapel Street, High Street and High Street East stocking everything from nuts and bolts, pots and pans, to fireplaces and sink units. Mr Kirman came from Richmond, North Yorkshire, and in the early years he employed one assistant, Frank Buttrick, and an errand boy. In 1910 Mr Kirman employed Charlie Burgess, who later became manager and a director of the company.

A boot repairers at 162 Ashby High Street in the 1920s with Frank Wilkins (right) and Bert Wilkins (left) outside their shop.

The shop window of D.W.Todd on the corner of High Street and Ravendale Street, Scunthorpe, currently occupied by Freeman, Hardy and Willis. The centre window sign boasts New Laid Eggs and Fresh Farm Butter collected from Farms Daily. The two oval signs read: 'Our Cheshire Cheese is Perfect' and 'We Are Noted For Bacon.' In the lower part of the window strips read: 'Selected Breakfast Bacon' and 'Finest Quality Smoked.' Packs of Sinclair's Snowflake pure lard are priced at 9d and there are a variety of cheeses on display. The sign to the left of the window says: 'This Window has been specially dressed, 1922 Grocers Exhibition and Market, Royal Agricultural Hall, London. September 16 to 22.' Many older Scunthonians and natives of Brigg will recall grocer's shops run by David Todd. The family originated from Messingham where Coates Todd was village blacksmith with a shop in Cross Tree Lane.

T. Fisher's butcher's shop at 72/74 High Street, Scunthorpe, took a pride in its eye-catching window displays, and this one, of January, 1925, was supervised by R.A.Blair.

David Todd's grocer's shop in Oswald Road, Scunthorpe, during the 1930s. From the left: Cyril Todd, Jim Bywater, manager Mr Dent, unknown, Wilf Watson and Eric Algar.

The building of the Scunthorpe Co-op's Ashton House in High Street, on the corner of Clark Street, in the late 1920s. The building was opened by Frederick Bond on July 5, 1930. Mr Bond was secretary of the Scunthorpe Co-operative Society Ltd.

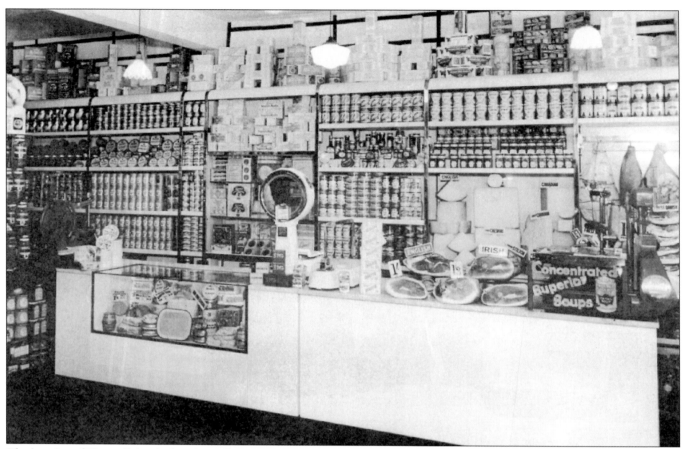

The interior of Henry Evison's shop in Wells Street, Scunthorpe, opposite to the then Trinity Methodist Church. The shop was first rented by the Gunsons in the 1930s. They previously had a shop in Manley Street.

A typically posed picture outside the premises of J.C.Lee, the chemist and stationer, in George Street, Barton. The premises are still a chemist shop.

A view of High Street, Scunthorpe, looking west prior to town centre re-development with Melia's shop on the corner of Market Hill. The tall building (centre right) is Trinity Methodist Church.

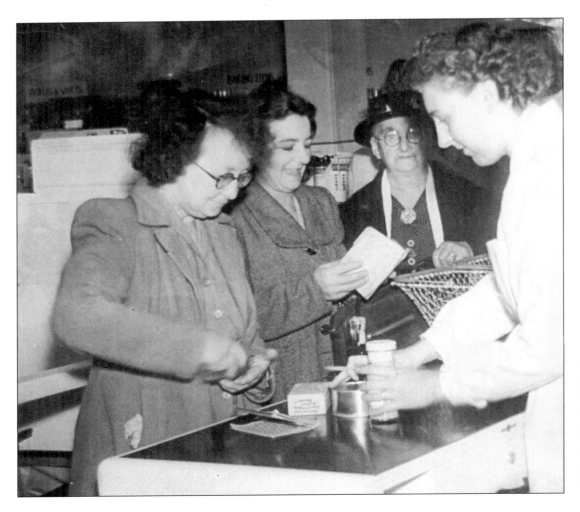

The Co-op central grocery in High Street, Scunthorpe, went self-service on September 19, 1949. Today we take this way of shopping for granted; then it was revolutionary.

Offering everything from knitting wool to bras, Walter Parker (extreme left), a very prominent and active member of Brigg Chamber of Trade, was in partnership as Parker and Cladingbowl in Wrawby Street, Brigg, for many years.

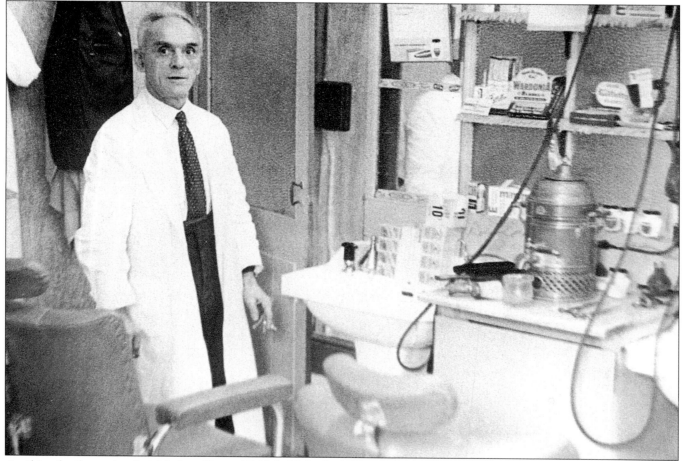

Anything for the weekend, sir? Sydney Howard Frith in his barber's shop on Ashby Broadway.

Personal Memories

'Mr Barton' looks back — Recollections of Ted Appleyard

The end of an era as Ted Appleyard of Barton stands on New Holland pier the day that the ferry stopped plying its trade across the river (June 24, 1981).

BARTON councillor Ted Appleyard comes from a family of shopkeepers and he can still fondly recall happy childhood days at the heart of a close family.

Grandma Mary Chapman who lived on Newport, Barton, the same street where Ted and his family lived, ran a fruit and sweet shop where the Overton Court flats stand now.

On Saturday Ted's mother used to to pull the fruit and veg cart around the Waterside and Ings Lane area with the help of Grandma's horse Tommy.

Ted recalls that Tommy, who was also pressed into service as the fire horse, was quite a character in his own right.

A gentle Welsh cob by nature who would allow the Appleyard boys to ride bareback on him, it was quite a different matter when it came to get him out of the stable.

The family worked hard six days a week but Sundays were special for a number of reasons. Grandma Chapman was astute enough to run her fruit and sweet business but, unable to read or write, looked forward to Ted's visits to help her with the Bible.

There were also family walks along the Humber bank to the former cement works (in the area of Reeds Hotel) where Uncle Bob worked, to watch him light the kilns.

In those early days Ted and his family lived in a house owned by Overton Wass, a well-known local shopkeeper.

"On Mondays my mother used to pay 2s 6d rent and 2s 6d into a club which would pay for

Former Royal Navy Petty Officer Ted Appleyard stands proudly at Barton's War Memorial following the annual Remembrance Day service.

clothes and the like," he said.

In those days life was conducted to a time-table almost unheard of these days.

"Friday was fish and chip day – one of each from Ada Headley's on Newport was 3d," said Ted. "Mum and Dad shared the fish and my two brothers and I had the chips with bread and butter."

The Saturday morning train brought to town the *Hull and Lincolnshire Times* and on Saturday evening outside the Oxford Cinema, the *Grimsby Evening Telegraph* could be bought for 1d and the sports paper for 2d.

"Anyone delivering weekly papers received the princely sum of one penny for each dozen delivered."

Ted was a pupil at Church School and when he left he went to join his father at the Hall's Barton Ropery.

Ted's great-great-grandfather was the first foreman there and each generation of the family after that found employment there.

At the age of 14 years Ted was employed as 'stake lad' – ensuring the ropes were at the correct tension when the ropes were spun – for the princely sum of 10s.

He later joined Elswick Hopper cycle works at the corner of Brigg Road and Castledyke South making packing crates for three half-pence a crate.

In 1937 he joined the Royal Navy and returned home 12 years later with his bride Madge whom he had married in 1947 after serving on *HMS Courageous* with her brother Bill.

His return to 'Civvy Street' saw a return once more to the Ropery, mixing tar and dye for the ropes and he stayed there until 1957, having opened his florist and grocery store on Bowmandale three years before.

For many years Ted's shop was the corner shop for the residents of the Bowmandale estate selling everything from food to paraffin as well as flowers.

Ted was elected to the Urban District

Ted Appleyard receives his long service award from the then Mayor of Glanford Borough Council, Coun John Wardle. Looking on is Glanford's chief executive David Cameron.

Council in 1962 and served as chairman in 1967-68.

He was elected on to Glanford Borough Council and Barton Town Council in 1974 and was Town Mayor in 1979-80. He represented the town and low villages on Humberside from 1980 and was elected to North Lincolnshire Council in 1995.

He has also been a member of the Humber Bridge Board and the Humberside Airport's Board.

Barton Councillor Ted Appleyard (centre) joins in the Queen's Silver Jubilee celebrations of 1977 with the residents of Grange Avenue, Barton.

Streets Ahead

This Scunthorpe cottage once stood on the corner of today's Oswald Road and Station Road (previously Water Lane). Today it is one of the busiest areas of the steel town in terms of road traffic – yet not even a pony and trap is in sight in this turn-of-the-century view.

The Crown Hotel at Ashby would on occasions provide accommodation for 'unusual' guests as with this 'lady' who is thought to be a drag artist on her way to the Palace Theatre in Cole Street, Scunthorpe. The plump lady in black, on the right, is believed to be Barbara Morley who married Slater Espin of School Road, Ashby, who had a fruit business which involved him visiting streets with a horse and cart.

Still popular today with Brigg people looking for somewhere to enjoy a quiet stroll, Cadney Road – seen here *c.*1920 – hugs the bank of the Old River Ancholme and is flanked by an avenue of fine trees. Proctor's yard is to the left.

High Street, Scunthorpe, around 1920, demonstrating that pedestrianised thoroughfares were just as popular with shoppers then as they are now.

George Street, Barton, in the 1920s. 'Anyone for ices?' might well have been the question posed by the vendor with his cold box. Many of them cycled round North Lincolnshire towns and villages and found a ready market – especially among the younger element.

Messingham Road, Bottesford, is hardly recognisable today from this 1930s view. Now there are houses on both sides of the street and it is a very busy thoroughfare in a place which has mushroomed from a quaint village to the second largest town in our area, behind Scunthorpe.

This view is looking up Scunthorpe High Street from the Ravendale Street junction and features the National Provincial Bank sub branch, the main one being at the bottom of Scunthorpe High Street, which moved to the Ravendale Street site after the featured bank premises were demolished in 1935 and replaced by a new building. The old main office in High Street became the council offices.

The Frances Street junction with Scunthorpe High Street. The street with Munro's dress shop canopies on the corner was previously named Cemetery Road as it led to Scunthorpe cemetery. To the fore of the photograph on the left would have been Baguleys carpet shop.

Frodingham Road, Crosby, with Holy Souls' Roman Catholic church on the right. The church was built and consecrated in 1911.

Generations of Scunthorpe area youngsters have thronged the streets in December to catch their first glimpse of Santa. Although today he usually drops in with a little help from the internal combustion engine, in 1951 things were still more traditional – a horse taking him down the High Street from Britannia Corner.

Hardly recognisable in view of today's rows of offices, this is Oswald Road, Scunthorpe, during the 1950s with the Majestic cinema (centre, left) just about the only remaining landmark.

Prefab houses – built to help with the post-war housing crisis – proved to be a big success in North Lincolnshire, offering many people their first taste of 'mod cons' like a fridge. Here we see Coronation celebrations being enjoyed in Warwick Road, Scunthorpe, in 1953. The number of youngsters in the picture just goes to demonstrate the post-1945 Baby Boom.

Wrawby Street, Brigg, playing host to the centuries-old horse fair in the 1950s, gypsies having travelled hundreds of miles to parade their livestock

bid for a bargain. Down to just a couple of horses a few years ago it has now been re-established and draws big crowds in early August.

Bridge Street, Brigg, in the late 1950s. Note the old Yarborough Hunt pub on the left, next to the premises of well-known firm Peacock and Binnington. Dunham's bakers (right) is still going today.

Father O'Hanlon, former Brigg parish priest, admiring the road named in his honour in the town in the 1960s. He looks suitably humble.

Crowle market place *c.*1965. The Morris Minor awaits the return of its owner, while a Bedford van (with sliding doors) busies itself on deliveries.

Not a hippy in sight although Flower Power was gripping the western world and The Beatles were at the height of their fame when this picture was taken looking down Scunthorpe High Street in 1967. Note the elderly van belonging to the well-known S and G Stores and the fact that a lorry carrying steel was then allowed down the town's main thoroughfare.

Broadway and Ashby High Street in the late 1960s. The building which housed the Co-op stores on Broadway, just off the photograph to the left, was built around 1957. In earlier years the area of the photograph in front of the parking bays to the left was occupied by cottages and behind them was a row of terrace houses known locally as Long Row, which were at right angles to the High Street. Their gardens stretched upwards towards Modder Street and gave open views from the High Street to Bottesford. Today's High Street beyond Modder Street led to the old cornmill at Ashby Turn and was called Mill Road. The new buildings to the right of the bus replaced Mill Road Club and its bowling green. On the corner of Collum Gardens was Rowbottom's chip shop and a row of shops including Bibby's and Espin's (replaced by the council offices) and off the photograph to the right would be the Globe/Roxy cinema, now the Malt Shovel.

High Ridge Filling Station, Scunthorpe, in the early 1970s when almost all garages offered stamps as an incentive to motorists. Pink or Green Shield stamps were stuck into books and, when filled, exchanged for gifts.

Buildings & Landmarks

All the pupils of Worlaby School seem to have been roused to pose for the Edwardian photographer.

Epworth Wesley Memorial Church, built in 1888. John and Charles Wesley, the founders of Methodism, were born in Epworth in 1703 and 1708. Their parents Samuel and Susanna Wesley had arrived in 1695 after he was appointed rector of Epworth. The Old Rectory was rebuilt after a fire in 1709. The church was built in 1888 by order of the 1882 Methodist Conference with donations flowing in from Methodists worldwide. Today both the church and old rectory draw visitors from around the world.

The elegant façade of Temple Bellwood, near Belton, which was demolished in the early 1970s. The site in early times was occupied by Celts who who elected Druids (priests) and held Beltane (a festival) in the groves of oaks, hence the names of Belton and Bel-wood. A history on the Temple noted: 'Here were also housed the people who were to be offered as Human Sacrifice in the Oak Grove which was regarded as the Supreme God. The chief Druid who would already have sent the Druids to inspect the land and spy out the worthless, would announce Beltane, a festival of sacrifice.' In 1144 King Stephen gave Belwood to the Knights of Templars who, in 1327, were granted permission by Edward III to form a monastic institution on the site. They razed to the ground the old buildings of the priests and cut down all the oaks in the Grove, thereby destroying the Temple and religion of Oak and Druid. The building later passed to the Knights Templars. The Temple building was renovated about 1865. It was, for a time, St Paul's High School for boys and during World War One was a hostel for Borstal boys.

The crumbling edifice of the once grand Temple Bellwood.

Barrow Hall in the snow around 1906. Records mention a building on the site as early as 1563 but the current building has parts going back to the 17th century with major additions in 1789. It was in the Uppleby family from 1746 until to the middle of this century. It has housed a farming college, a children's home and is now a residential home.

Clayfield Road council school in Scunthorpe opened in 1912. The road on which it stands was later renamed Doncaster Road. The building was demolished in 1998 to make way for the Lidl store. Prior to then it was known as Ancholme House and was part of North Lindsey College.

Fire destroyed Appleby Hall in 1933. It was never rebuilt. Appleby was the home of the Winn family who came originally from Gwydir in North Wales. It was bought from Stephen Anderson of Manby Hall, Broughton, around 1650 by Sir George Winn. The Hall was started in 1700 for use as a shooting lodge by the Winn family who also had Nostell Priory near Wakefield. It was enlarged in 1750 and considerably extended in the 1850s following the marriage of Rowland Winn and Harriet Dumaresq of Haverholme Hall. The extensions provided 30 to 40 rooms, servant's quarters and stables. Rowland Winn began a systematic search for ironstone in the area in 1858 and the subsequent discovery and extraction of reserves spawned the iron and steel industry in Scunthorpe. Rowland Winn eventually moved to Nostell Priory, on becoming Lord St Oswald in 1885, and after his death in 1893 his widow moved back to Appleby Hall where she lived till her death in 1926, followed by her daughter Emily in 1927. The Hall was then used on odd occasions for shooting parties with fires lit beforehand to air the building. It is thought sparks from one of these started the blaze in 1933.

The Gate House at Appleby Hall. Somehow the inclusion of the elderly bearded 'local' adds, rather than detracts, from the view of this quaint little building.

The Keeper's Lodge on Lord Oswald's Estate between Appleby and Broughton. The shooting lodge was built in the 19th century and used by the Winn family of Appleby Hall and Nostell Priory. The gothic style building, roofed in slate, houses an octagonal reception room with a vaulted ceiling, which was used as a dining room, with pine octagonal furniture to match. The internal doors echo the windows in shape. The building is now called Springwood Lodge and is sometimes known as Appleby Cottage.

Appleby Hall after the fire on September 15, 1933.

Historic Brumby Hall, Scunthorpe. Reference was made to a hall at Brumby as far back as 1390 when Robert Wasslyn of Wascelin and his wife Johanna were granted a licence for a private chapel within the manor of Burneby. The present day building, seen here around 1920, is of more modern construction with parts dating back to the 17th century with a mixture of Georgian and Victorian features. The Hall is reputedly haunted by a lady in white who, it is said, leaves the tower at midnight and walks along Brumby Wood Lane.

The Wortley House Hotel, Rowland Road, Scunthorpe, c.1920. It is scarcely recognisable as today's well-known establishment, the ugly wooden fence having long gone.

The old workhouse at Brigg. Work started in 1835 and was completed in 1837. It was not a workhouse in the Dickensian sense but served as a home for the poor and destitute and was administered by a Board of Guardians. Part of the site of the old workhouse is now occupied by the Rosecroft residential home.

A pony and trap ready for use at Winterton Hall, with a small dog waiting for his masters' voice.

The Primitive Methodist Connexion Chapel which stood in High Street, Scunthorpe, on the site of today's shops – Superdrug, Our Price and Evans. It was built in the 1890s and closed in 1935. The old chapel was bought by Reginald Heslam and converted into a high-class furniture store called Heslam House. He retired in 1961.

The Palace Theatre in Cole Street, Scunthorpe, which later became The Savoy, The Classic and Essoldo cinemas. Well-known stripper, Phyllis Dixie appeared here, as did Hughie Green of *Opportunity Knocks* fame.

Latterly the Poundstretcher store, this striking building in Cole Street, Scunthorpe, is seen here in summer 1978 as home to the Classic Cinema. The building, which started life as the Palace Theatre, is scheduled for demolition as part of further town centre redevelopment.

Redbourne Primary School, built in 1931, closed at the end of the 1960s. The head of the school in the 1950s was Mabel Watmough. The style of architecture, particularly the wooden verandah, was employed on many North Lincolnshire schools. Many could also boast rosebeds and flagpoles.

Records show Walcot Hall, which was originally supported from farm rents, was in existence before 1649 and that it was refurbished in 1700 and again in 1800 when Thomas Goulton extended it and had the gardens laid out. The old kitchens at the hall were demolished in the 1960s and the third storey of the building was also removed. It is now a private residence.

This view of Cole Street/Wells Street crossroads with Scunthorpe High Street features Trinity Methodist Church. The foundation stone for the church was laid in 1898. The chapel opened in 1900 and was demolished in 1960. The buildings on the right, with Harry Jacobs' shop, were demolished for town centre redevelopment in the 1960s.

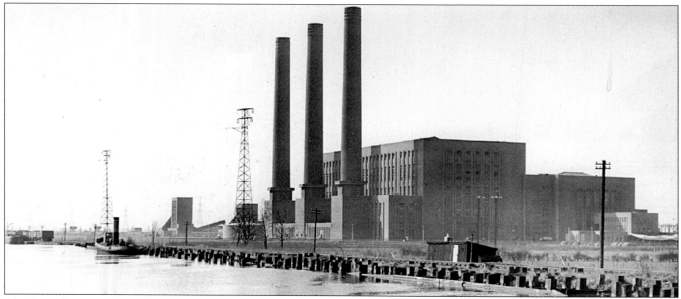

The three chimneys of Keadby coal-fired power station reflected here in the waters of the Stainforth and Keadby Canal, prior to their demolition in 1991. The decision to build a station in Keadby was taken in 1946 and the power station with a maximum installed capacity of 360,000 kilowatts commenced operating in April, 1952 and was officially opened by Sir Henry Self, the deputy chairman

(administration), Central Electricity Generating Board, on April 20, 1956. The station, on a 181 acre site, was closed in 1984. Work on a gas and steam combined station on the site, with 680 megawatt capacity, started in 1992. It went into full commercial operation in January, 1996.

Scotter Primitive Methodist church, built in 1819 and sold to the Methodist New Connexion in 1849, closed in 1948 and was demolished some 30 years ago.

Kirton Lindsey market place in 1967 with the Town Hall dominating the view. Being C-Reg, the Mini was almost brand new.

The Regal Cinema, Crowle, which opened on September 6, 1937, closed on August 20, 1970. The widespread arrival of television was the cause of the closure of many of the regions cinemas in the 1960s and 1970s, Brigg's Grand closing at about the same time as the Isle of Axholme venue.

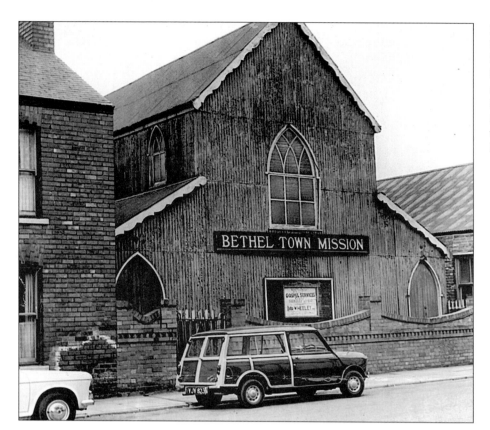

Nicknamed The Tin Tabernacle, the Bethel Town Mission was in Gilliatt Street, Scunthorpe, offering Gospel Services, among others. The church had originally been on the corner of High Street and Gilliatt Street, before being moved to the site featured. Many of us will remember the old wood-panelled Mini Estate car with affection.

Lindsey County Fire Brigade at Scawby Grove in the late 1960s. Ambulancemen also stood by as attempts are made to help down those who have taken to the roof. Originally an imposing private residence, The Grove was transformed to house youngsters being helped by Social Services.

Ashby Infants School in 1971. On March 31 Mrs Eva Sewell (head) and two children, Diane Burgess and Ian Turtle, attended a Save the Children Fund reception at Newark at which they were presented to Princess Anne. The following month Mrs Sewell retired, having been head for 19 of her 25 years at the school. Immediately behind Eva Sewell to the left of those in the doorway is Betty Brocklesby with Minnie Kirmond and Anna Glossop.

Like many Scunthorpe buildings, what is now Henry Afrika's on Doncaster Road has enjoyed several changes of usage and ownership. Back in 1981 it was Tiffany's and owned by the national leisure concern, Mecca. And a Mecca it certainly was for fun-seekers! It was also the ABC and Ritz cinemas and at one stage housed an ice rink.

St John's Church, Scunthorpe, and surrounding area from the top of Crosby flats in the early 1970s. Appleby-Frodingham steelworks smoke

...ay in the distance. Work on Scunthorpe Library started in March 1972 and was completed in July 1974.

Humber Ferry

A fine 1944 view of the *Lincoln Castle* ferry crossing the River Humber. The first ferry is said to have been established way back in 1316, at the request of the burgesses of Hull, and ran between the Yorkshire town and Barton. New Holland was a more attractive proposition because of the position of sandbanks and tides and gained major importance in the 1840s with the arrival of the railways. The ferry, through a variety of craft including the *Tattershall Castle*, the *Killingholme* and the *Brocklesby*, gave super service to passengers and vehicles. But it all came to an end with the completion of the Humber Bridge in 1981.

Despite being battered by spray from the River Humber below, this antique lamp standard on the side of New Holland Pier would have offered a little light in the gloom in the early years of the 20th century.

Humber Ferry, the *Tattershall Castle*, still operating, despite World War Two, in 1944. The vessel is now moored on the Thames Embankment, London. Its sister ship the, *Wingfield Castle*, is moored at Hartlepool where they were both built.

Cattle on board a Humber Ferry at New Holland. The last ferry to cross the Humber was the *Farringford* on June 24, 1981.

An atmospheric shot of the New Holland Pier sign in the foreground and the Humber Ferry sailing away to Hull in the background. Signs like this change hands for a tidy sum among today's collectors.

The sun was setting on the Humber Ferry in more ways than one when this picture was taken shortly before the service came to a halt. The vessel is now a restaurant moored in Grimsby's Alexandra Dock.

Although the ever-growing use of family cars was to prove the death knell for the Humber Ferry, they were providing a useful income for the river service in 1973 when this moment was recorded for posterity.

Bridges

The County Bridge in Brigg, spanning the Old River Ancholme, seen in the 1950s. This picture shows the structure in its original form with the stone balustrades, later replaced by wooden and then metal rails. With the introduction of Brigg's long-awaited inner relief road by-pass, in recent times, the bridge has been spared the thousands of heavy lorries which once trundled over it every week.

Talked about for decades as a way of linking the communities either side of the great estuary, the Humber Bridge began to take shape in 1973 with the foundations for the towers and anchorages and was finally opened eight years later. The Queen gave the structure royal approval by making the official opening and The Red Arrows roared overhead as thousands of local people turned out for a day to remember. When completed it was the longest single-span suspension bridge in the world at 1,410 metres (4,626 feet). The tolls, of course, were, and still are, unpopular, while the huge bridge debt has long been a political hot potato. But whatever your views on that topic, the bridge certainly beats waiting for the Humber Ferry or driving round to the north bank by Goole. This picture shows the Humber Bridge in the early stages of construction.

The Humber Bridge in the early stages of construction. Using a system of continuous concreting, called slip forming, the southern towers steadily rose above the supporting caissons, built into the river bed.

Seven-year-old Wager and his handler, Sgt Charles Firth, of Securicor, guarding the Humber Bridge site as the monster construction takes shape.

Members of the Humber Bridge Board from the North and the South Banks meet in the centre of the Humber Bridge, just prior to its official opening in 1981. Centre is Councillor Ted Appleyard, from Barton, with his own model of the bridge, in flowers.

Winteringham County Primary School pupils with their banner and flags await the arrival of the Queen for the opening of the Humber Bridge.

World famous display team The Red Arrows reach for the skies at the opening of the Humber Bridge by the Queen on July 17, 1981.

Cheering crowds at the opening of the Humber Bridge in July, 1981.

A panoramic view of the Humber Bridge, illuminated at night, taken soon after its official opening.

The River Trent was first bridged at Keadby in 1864 by the South Yorkshire Railway but the swing bridge became dangerous after half a century of valued service and was replaced by the current structure, carrying road and rail traffic, erected 200 feet downstream from the old one. The present bridge, The King George V, was to the Scherzer 'rolling lift' design, pivoted at one end and counterweighted. The fact that the bridge could lift meant that the waterway was not obstructed in the centre by the supporting tower. Yet there have been many occasions when craft have struck the bridge. Similarly, in hot weather, the expansion of metal has caused problems. Permission to build the first bridge was obtained by an Act of Parliament in July 1861. The first engine across the bridge was driven by Thomas Woodruff Woodley in May 1864 when there was only a single track. The bridge was strengthened before the first passenger trains. The bridge was designed by Charles Bartholomew and was 484ft long by 25ft. The swing section was 160ft long.

The imposing King George V bridge at Keadby in the lifting position, to allow river traffic to pass safely by along the Trent. The first train to cross it left Althorpe station at 10.35am on May 21, 1916 and Joshua Slowan, the driver of the first passenger train to cross the Trent on the original bridge, took place of honour on the engine, at the age of 76. In 1926 the bridge was improved by removing a footpath and widening the road. A new footbridge was built for pedestrians. Despite strong opposition from shipping, river concerns and Gainsborough Urban District Council, an Act of Parliament authorised the 3,600 ton bridge's huge lifting span to become fixed in the down position from April 1, 1956.

Keadby Bridge in the 1970s, showing the massive counterbalance arrangement. The structure became known as 'The Bridge of Sighs' because of congestion to road-users, but the situation was eased by the opening of the M180, which took away a good deal of traffic.

A fine bird's-eye view of the M180 crossing the River Ancholme, near Brigg, by way of a concrete bridge, opened in September, 1977. The Castle-thorpe Corner to Barnetby Top stretch of motorway brought real relief to the people of Brigg and Wrawby, whose streets had become increasingly clogged by an average 18,000 cars and lorries each day. The M180 became Humberside's first completed motorway. Also visible on this picture is the bridge taking the A18 over the New River Ancholme, near to Yarborough Mills (now demolished). Running away to the left is the Old River Ancholme, lined with craft belonging to Glanford Boat Club members.

Railways

An historic day for North Lincolnshire in 1867 with the opening of the original Frodingham (Scunthorpe) railway station. The arrival of the railways meant that the area's iron and steel industry could really take off, with raw materials being moved in more easily and the finished products taken out to feed the booming Victorian manufacturing industries. They, in turn, sent their wares throughout an Empire on which the sun never set.

The first train along the North Lindsey Light Railway in 1906 pauses at Thealby. From a postcard sent on the very first day. There were many ambitious plans for this line, including links with the North Bank. But they came to nothing. The closure of local ironstone mines and Normanby Park steelworks were further major blows, but part of the line still remains for freight, including waste going to the tip at Winterton. Flixborough Wharf also continues to be an important port for the steel trade.

Work under way on the loco shed at New Holland in the early part of the 20th century, the contractors being Stamp and Son of Brigg Road, Barton.

A map showing the Lincolnshire railway network at its zenith in the 1930s. Note the rural lines criss-crossing the Isle of Axholme and the North Lindsey Light Railway running from Scunthorpe to Whitton and Winteringham.

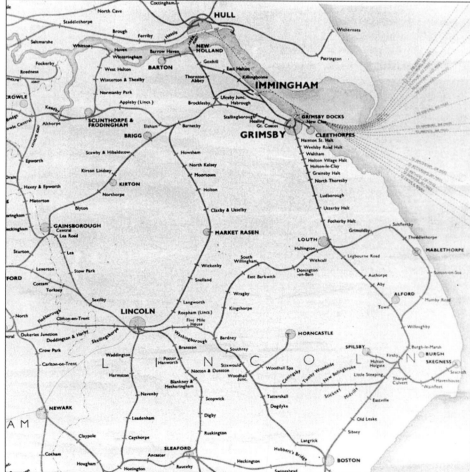

A misty day in Scunthorpe in 1938 with the busy mainline crossing over Dawes Lane. The large signalbox in the background is Trent Junction, on the outskirts of the town. It disappeared as part of modernisation in the early 1970s which saw a modern power box and colour light signals replacing the old signal cabins with lever frames and semaphore signals.

The wheel has turned full circle as far as railways are concerned. First there were private companies, then nationalisation in 1948, and now private companies have returned to the fold once again. Back in the early decades of the century, 'private owner wagons' as they were known were to be seen throughout North Lincolnshire. And here we see workmen in front of a Frodingham Iron and Steel Company wagon. Judging by the saw being held by one of those on the back row this gang was involved in repairs.

A fine sunny day in Barnetby during the 1950s as a WD Austerity 2-8-0 drifts past with a rake of empty mineral wagons. The path in the foreground was known in the village as the Cinder Trod.

Being an engine driver was once the dream of every youngster, or so they say. Frodingham loco depot in Scunthorpe, though, was not the most glamorous of places to work, being without express passenger duties. Most of the footplatemen had to be content with slow freight duties, often at night to avoid getting in the way of more important traffic. Steam locos were rugged pieces of machinery but needed lots of maintenance if they were to perform to anything like full capacity. This is passed fireman Derrick Soulby carrying out some routine topping up at the local shed during the late 1950s. Those in the footplate grades started as cleaners, then became cleaners who could fill in as firemen, when required. The next stage was to become a full-time fireman, then a passed fireman (a stoker who could also drive in times of shortage). Reaching the rank of driver could take several decades of slow progress up the promotion ladder.

With road, rail and water transport coming together at Keadby Bridge, over the River Trent, this spot has long been a favourite with North Lincs photographers. This was May, 1956 and Frodingham-based 04 class 2-8-0 No. 63696 rumbles onto the bridge as a family car heads in the other direction.

During the late 1950s B1 class 4-6-0 No. 61150 arrives at Barnetby – a small village but a very important railway centre for North Lincolnshire, to this day.

Old meets new at Scunthorpe station in the early 1960s as a visiting Stanier 2-8-0 returns home to West Yorkshire while an 0-6-0 diesel shunter goes about its duties in the west yard on the right of picture. The signal box disappeared in the 1970s.

Children today would recognise this loco as being Percy, from the *Thomas the Tank Engine* stable. However, this is no fictional creation but an actual working loco seen moving locally mined ironstone in Scunthorpe in the early 1960s.

Steam locomotive 70040 *Clive of India* drifts through Appleby *c.*1962. Half-a-dozen of the powerful British Railways Britannia class locos were allocated to North Lincolnshire in the early 1960s – a real treat for local trainspotters, more used to mundane freight engines. This particular engine was withdrawn from Carlisle Kingmoor depot in April, 1967 and cut up for scrap with years of useful life still in it – a sad waste of taxpayers' money.

Barton railway station on the day after Dr Beeching announced plans to close it in 1963 as part of his national scheme to axe scores of lines and services. However, the station survives to this day, albeit without the once-extensive buildings. The diesel shunter was one of the earliest of its type to work on British Railways, perhaps explaining why its design included a chimney which would not have looked out of place on a steam loco.

Trainspotting was regarded as a perfectly normal and harmless pastime for much of this century and only in relatively recent years have 'the Boys in Anoraks' been branded as odd, if not downright peculiar. Thousands of North Lincolnshire youngsters used to sit by the lineside, record the numbers of passing locos in their notebooks and then copy them out later into the trainspotters' bible, *The Ian Allan ABC of British Locomotives*. It was a very cheap hobby. The more organised spotters formed themselves into clubs and societies and even ran their own special trains, as is the case in this picture. It shows Frodingham-based K1 class 2-6-0 No. 62035 with a Railway Enthusiasts' Club special train made up of 10 brake vans on the North Lindsey Light Railway at Winterton and Thealby station in 1963.

This train was hired by the North Axholme School at Crowle to say farewell to the Axholme Joint Railway on April 1, 1965. It was a very slow ride for the schoolchildren over one of North Lincolnshire's most rural of rural lines – but a memorable one.

An historic day for Scunthorpe area railways… February 26, 1966 and the last booked steam working prepares to leave Frodingham loco depot. WD Austerity 2-8-0 No. 90465 was manned by driver E.Jarman and fireman C.E.Jarman and was returning home to West Yorkshire. Some steam locos continued to work into Scunthorpe from the Leeds and Wakefield areas until the following spring. The Austerities were very rugged locos and more than 700 saw service with British Railways but not one was preserved. The engine pictured was based at Normanton shed and sent for scrap in early 1967.

World famous steam loco *Flying Scotsman* approaching Brigg Road bridge in the late 1960s at the head of an enthusiasts' special. This loco used to haul top expresses between London King's Cross station and Scotland and was saved from the breaker's yard in 1963 by enthusiast Alan Pegler. On its few appearances in North Lincolnshire during the late 1960s *Flying Scotsman* drew huge crowds and one of the authors well remembers spending hours on Barnetby station, in the pouring rain and driving wind, awaiting its arrival – many hours later than scheduled.

An unusual view of Wrawby Junction, *c.*1970. This huge signalbox – the third largest lever-controlled one in the country with 137 – has handled the traffic for three routes, from Cleethorpes to Lincoln, Sheffield and Scunthorpe for many decades. In the days of steam the junction could boast its own turntable and was a very important place for iron ore traffic from the Midlands.

Track modernisation underway to the railway network in Scunthorpe in 1972, in the light of the multi-million pound Anchor development by British Steel. This picture was taken near Yard No.1 signalbox.

Personal Memories

The Demise of Steam
by former Scunthorpe loco driver Roy Cross

Former Scunthorpe locoman Roy Cross on the footplate of one of his beloved steam locos.

THE view from the messroom window, looking in the direction of the coal road at Frodingham steam shed, in the early 1960s, will remain with me for the rest of my life.

Four steam locomotives were in the process of being coupled together to be towed away for scrap.

I took on this scene with mixed feelings.

Firstly, the industry had to move with the times to compete with other forms of transport; I accepted that.

Secondly, there was a sentiment of uneasiness. After all, steam had been with us for a hundred years.

Thirdly a feeling of sadness came over me as I thought about the happy times spent on steam and the camaraderie which existed between the men involved.

The question I asked myself was: How would I cope personally?

I buckled down and studied hard and moved with the times.

The following ten years were bland compared with the years prior to diesel electrics.

One must remember that the rostering on steam was vastly different – driver and fireman were together for 12 months until things were altered in October.

This pairing of men produced lasting friendships.

The driver, no matter who his fireman was, would always stand by him.

I've been with colleagues who, for years after our pairing, would bring flowers for my wife each Christmas, and presents for my children.

But that sort of nicety nearly disappeared with steam, as men became isolated with the 'single manning' of diesels.

The messroom was the place where this change in attitudes took place.

No matter what the topic of conversation was, it invariably deviated round to steam experiences.

That was all right for us old steam hands, but there were new footplatemen with us who had never been on a steam locomotive.

It was no fault of theirs, but they soon got fed up of listening to stories from days of yore, and offered to sweep up the ashes and coal from the messroom floor after a session of steam day yarns!

But, in my opinion, this proved just how much the men missed steam days.

Steam had only been displaced by diesel for a couple of years when this Brush Type 4 diesel left Scunthorpe at the head of a steel train in December, 1968. A Brush Type 2 and a 350bhp shunter can also been seen.

Road Transport

One of North Lincolnshire's best-known motor dealers, G.H.Layne, offered a full service – car sales, painting and repairs – on a site in Bigby Street, Brigg. These days the premises house a snooker club.

Joseph Hornsby, of the famous Scunthorpe family firm, poses proudly beside a 1924 Garford bus.

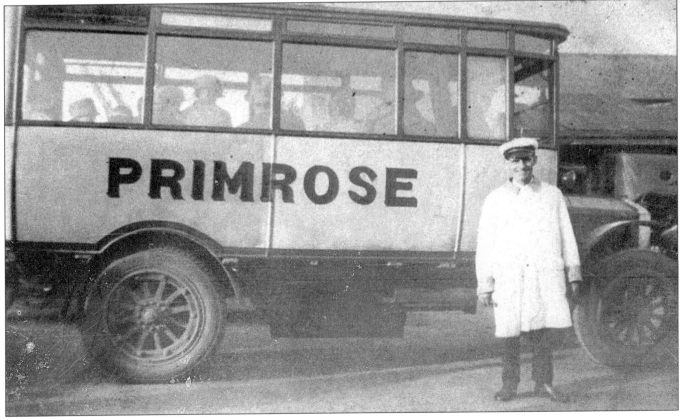

Council road foreman Amos Hornsby with bicycle during the building of the Kingsway/Queensway Scunthorpe Bypass Road, around 1933. The engineer and surveyor for the road was Mr Walter Farrar and the chairman of the highway committee of the then Scunthorpe and Frodingham Urban District Council was Coun John Tomlinson. When built the road cut through open countryside with Crosby, Frodingham and Scunthorpe to the North and Brumby, Ashby, Bottesford and Yaddlethorpe to the south. The approved estimated cost of the works was £122,454 with the Ministry of Transport providing 85 per cent of the cost, Lindsey County Council six and a quarter per cent and the Urban District Council eight and threequarters. It was opened by HRH Prince George on October 26, 1933.

The Lincolnshire Motor Co Ltd in Brigg Road, Scunthorpe, with St Johns' Parish church in the background. The photo was used in an advert in the *Scunthorpe Evening Telegraph* in March, 1957.

Steel and Iron Ore

Mining ironstone in the Scunthorpe area in Victorian times was back-breaking work, when mechanical aids were few and far between. Layers of earth had to be removed, then the iron-bearing rock blasted away before being put into wagons by teams of men with shovels and barrows.

Ironworks employees at John Lysaght's works in the early part of the 20th century. The casthouse floor can be seen in the distance – open to the elements on two sides, making working conditions even more unpleasant.

Joiners at Appleby-Frodingham steelworks in 1939. On the extreme left (front) is Billy Skinner of Old Crosby, George Marshall is third row back, second left. On the third row back, second from right, is Bob Duc; George Dickinson is third from the right of the second row back; and Eddie Chapman is on the extreme left of the second row back.

Hand-charging furnaces at Appleby-Frodingham in the early 1950s, just before this came to an end. It seems incredible that men had to shovel iron ore into these huge barrows, then manhandle them towards the top of the furnace and tip in the contents. Can there have been a more exacting manual job in the iron and steel industry?

Women found a host of previously men-only jobs in the shopfloor areas of the Scunthorpe steelworks during the war and many continued to work after the end of hostilities. This view from Appleby plate mills in 1953 features Val Weston, Olive Shadlock, Lorna Lewchuk, Margaret Fenwick, Beryl Barley and Eileen Barley.

A quiet moment in the ingot stockyard at John Lysaght's (Normanby Park) steelworks in 1955. Crane Driver Chris Smith, in the bowler hat, was also a well-known boxer. The slingers are H.Wilson, of Gurnell Street, Scunthorpe, and Harry McPheat.

The first cantilever stand ever to be constructed at a British football stadium went up at the Old Showground, home of Scunthorpe United, in 1958. And what an impressive structure it was, offering a view of the pitch uncluttered by pillars and posts. The East Stand was erected by United Steel Structural Company, the locally-based concern, but demolished in 1988 when the Iron sold their home for a supermarket development and moved to Glanford Park. Could there have been a case for the authorities declaring the structure a listed building? Not only was it the first of its kind but also part of Scunthorpe's steel heritage. Scunthorpe steel has found its way into grandstands at many of Britain's leading football grounds, including Liverpool's Anfield, Rangers' Ibrox and Nottingham Forest's City Ground. The cantilever stand replaced the old East Stand which was destroyed by fire on March 17, 1958, close to the end of a season in which the Iron won promotion to the old Second Division from the regionalised Third Division North.

Frodingham melting shop with its famous nine chimneys dominates the foreground of this late 1950s/early 1960s bird's-eye view of Appleby-Frodingham steelworks, Scunthorpe. The Four Queens blast-furnaces are on the right of the picture.

A dramatic representation of casting under way on
a blast-furnace in Scunthorpe.

Construction work under way on the massive Anchor steelworks project in Scunthorpe *c.*1970. The famous Four Queens blast-
furnaces are away in the distance. This may look like a lunar landscape but after a super effort by teams of contractors, the new Anchor
plant soon took shape, altering for ever the view along Brigg Road.

A look at the BOS steelmaking plant at the Anchor site, Scunthorpe, in May, 1972. It was taken from Brigg Road – beyond the official entrance to the site. That location is particularly relevant because a sign on the left announces: 'No photographs to be taken on this site – offenders' films will be confiscated'.

The Anchor steelworks under construction in Scunthorpe in the early 1970s. There was a strong argument at the time for siting any new steelworks on the coast, cutting out the expense of transporting raw materials inland to be processed and finished products the other way for export. But the British Steel Corporation decided to favour Scunthorpe with a multi-million pound investment, involving not only a BOS steelmaking plant but also bloom and billet and medium section mills, plus associated plant.

Anchor Village was a large community of portable buildings erected near to where the Morrisons superstore now stands at Ashby Ville. It was originally there to house workers involved on the huge construction site for the Anchor steelworks development. But, once that was complete in the early 1970s, many workers new to British Steel, when skilled labour was still in short supply, were housed in what became a hostel. A look at the huge array of keys for the different chalets, seen here in the reception area, gives an indication of the size of the site.

Scunthorpe suffered the worst disaster in the history of the British Steel Corporation on November 4, 1975. An explosion, centred on this molten iron-carrying torpedo ladle, claimed the lives of 11 workers and shocked the whole town. Hundreds of gallons of water found its way from the Queen Victoria blast-furnace cooling system into the top of the ladle, containing 175 tonnes of molten metal. When the torpedo was moved and the water and metal mixed, there was a huge explosion. A spokesman for British Steel described the scene, vividly, as being 'just like Dante's Inferno'. A disaster fund was established and a plaque subsequently erected as a memorial to those who died.

The memorial on the casthouse floor at Appleby-Frodingham to those who died in the 1975 Queen Victoria blast-furnace disaster.

Scunthorpe's most famous landmarks – The Four Queens, Bess, Mary, Anne and Victoria. The first two of the giant blast-furnaces came into being in the late 1930s and the latter two in the mid-1950s. Much modified, rebuilt and modernised they remain, despite their commissioning dates, very much part of British Steel today. This panoramic view dates from the late 1960s, soon after they passed from the ownership of Appleby-Frodingham to the newly established British Steel Corporation.

A fine bird's-eye view of Scunthorpe's Normanby Park steelworks, taken during the 1970s and showing the fully integrated works with its LD/AC steelmaking plant, blast-furnaces and mills. Some of it remains today but much of the site has been redeveloped for a variety of commercial and industrial uses as the Lysaght's Enterprise Park. A phoenix rising from the ashes!

The relighting of a Scunthorpe blast-furnace after relining and modifications taking many months was always a major event in the steelworks calendar. Here we see workers at the No.6 blast-furnace at Normanby Park, towards the end of its life in the 1970s.

New British Steel chairman, Sir Charles Villiers (right) being shown around the ironworks by Appleby blast-furnaces manager Keith Graham during a tour of the Scunthorpe complex in April, 1978. Keith was a very well-known local cricketer, playing for Normanby Park Works and also being a high-ranking official of the Lincolnshire League.

An historic picture as the temperature is taken before the sampling of the final steel cast at Normanby Park works in February, 1981. Closure came as part of the major steelworks cutbacks. BSC employees, past and present, joined together to witness the last rites and pay their respects to an old friend. On that final day blast-furnaceman Dick Holloway, of Whitestone Road, Scunthorpe, summed up what it was like to be a Lysaght's employee. "It was always a pleasure to come to work," he said. "We have come to expect this closure for the past 10 years, but it has still come as a shock. You get all tied up in a knot deep inside and then the feeling turns to anger." Acting general manager Frank Braithwaite said: "The workers here have been first class; in fact, second to none. But there were no options other than closure open to BSC in view of the circumstances. The steel tonnage required for this next year was too much for Teesside and Scunthorpe, so there had to be a reduction in general capacity or everything would have gone by the board."

Cutbacks in the steel industry in the late 1970s and early 1980s became a major political issue and here leading Labour Party left-winger Tony Benn (left) and National Union of Mineworkers' president Arthur Scargill (right) share the protest platform with local union leader George Teal of the Iron and Steel Trades Confederation. He worked at Normanby Park steelworks, as a vessel operator, for many years, and that entire plant was earmarked for closure by British Steel, then being streamlined by tough-talking BSC supremo Ian MacGregor. In a very famous quote, the then Mayor of Scunthorpe, Coun Fred Dring, described the announcement, in mid-December, 1980, of 4,100 job losses by the following March as 'Mr MacGregor's sick Christmas card'. And as the proposals for the total closure of Normanby Park and the No.1 rod mill were put to an angry meeting of about 100 trades union representatives, BSC's group director, Derek Saul, was greeted by boos and catcalls. Brigg and Scunthorpe Conservative MP, Michael Brown, supported 'Mac The Knife', saying the closures were in the long-term interests of survival. "Normanby Park has always had a question mark over it," he declared. "It is no use being sentimental over this."

Marchers in Scunthorpe, unhappy about cutbacks in steel jobs, passing Frodingham House – home of the local steelworks 'top brass' – during the bitter steel strike of 1979/1980. Among union chiefs leading from the front are George Teal (Iron and Steel Trades Confederation) and Albert Chudley (National Union of Blast-furnacemen). With overcapacity, overmanning, poor export prices and little demand, British Steel was looking to cut back, or streamline, in all areas – even at super centres like Scunthorpe. The unions and workers were unimpressed, knowing that the steel industry had traditionally enjoyed good times and bad and that profits would soon return. Why should this latest trough be any different? The end result was a lengthy strike – and a bitter one. With hindsight both sides in the dispute might argue that they were proved right. Within a few years the slimmed-down British Steel bounced back into profit, making millions to be enjoyed, in part, by its new shareholders. That pruning certainly safeguarded the future of Scunthorpe as a steeltown – but at a terrible cost to scores of families whose main source of income had been wiped out with the closure of Normanby Park, Redbourn and the ore mines.

Even viewed two decades after the event, this scene will be a sad one for many former Scunthorpe steelworkers. It shows one of the Redbourn blast-furnaces being felled in 1980. Elderly and of relatively small capacity, the Redbourn ironworks was one of the first areas earmarked for cutbacks, in an announcement in March, 1979. The furnacemen at the former Richard Thomas and Baldwin's plant were a close-knit community and the fact that their livelihoods were due to disappear came as a tragic blow.

This monster was just about as big as things got in the local ore mines. Weighing over 1,800 tonnes, British Steel's huge Rapier W1800 walking dragline, belonging to the ore mining branch, used its huge bucket to expose the ironstone layer, prior to blasting and quarrying. While at Winterton mine it moved 11.5 million cubic yards of overburden, leading to the production of 4.5 million tonnes of ironstone. By the time this picture was taken in 1980 ironstone mining in the Scunthorpe area was all but finished, British Steel finding it more economic to import ore from overseas, via the deep water port at Immingham.

Shift change time on the steelworks has always brought a great deal of traffic on to Scunthorpe's streets. Steelworkers used to go to work by bicycle – thousands of them – but that form of transport has gradually been overshadowed by cars, motorcycles and scooters. This picture, taken in 1980 at the North Lincoln Road entrance to Appleby-Frodingham, nicely contrasts people power and the internal combustion engine. In the background is the new power station, finished in the mid-1970s, central laboratories and Appleby coke ovens.

Personal Memories

Charlie Framp and the days of 'Dilly Ernie'

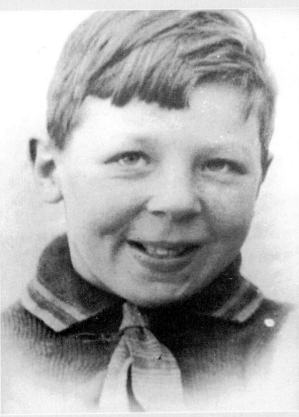

Charlie Framp of Belmont Street, Ashby, as a boy. He grew up in nearby Lindley Street.

Charlie Framp in retirement.

CHARLIE Framp was born in Lindley Street, Ashby, in 1922 and finally settled in neighbouring Belmont Street.

"The house in Lindley Street was the usual sort of terraced property. It had no gas, electricity or water and no bathroom or inside toilet," he recalls.

"Water was drawn from a shared well out the back; the bucket closet was at the bottom of the yard behind the pig sty. This was emptied weekly by a character we knew as 'Dilly' Ernie – always after dark.

"The Ashby countryside began with a cornfield no more than 30 or 40 yards from our front door – beyond that were grassy meadows all the way to Old Brumby in which cows grazed and buttercups, daisies and cowslips grew."

Charlie attended Ashby Infants, Juniors and Brumby Senior Boys School.

At the Infants, children wrote on wooden framed slates. Mrs Walmsley was headmistress.

At Ashby Boys a bell rang for 15 minutes to 9am. "If you weren't then in the school yard you were late and there by the gates would be old 'Chucky' Bramley, the headmaster, to fetch you a quick whack across the seat of your pants as you raced by him into the school yard."

On the outbreak of war in 1939 Charlie was working with his brother Ernie as an apprentice bricklayer with the Ashby firm of Green and Mackender.

"We built air-raid shelters at the schools and all over the town. When that work finished in 1940 the firm closed down for the duration."

He recalled families after the war living in abandoned Army camps. He and his wife Jean were delighted to be given the tenancy of a pre-fab on Kenilworth Road, Brumby, in 1948.

"In 1946 I obtained a job at the Redbourn works of Richard Thomas and Baldwin as a bricklayer – the work consisted mostly of building and repairing the company's seven open hearth furnaces.

"The hot repairs to a furnace – we called it 'fettling' – was hell's own job. The heat escaping from a hole in a furnace roof comes through it with all the speed of a bullet and so intense is it, if you let it, it will boil your eyes in their sockets.

"On such jobs I've known many a man's cap or his clothes catch fire when he'd reached a little too far into or over the heat – you could lose half a stone in weight in less than half a shift on jobs like that.

"Conditions almost anywhere on the steel-works could be dangerous – over the years I've known more than a few who have suffered death or serious injury there.

"I became shop steward for the bricklayers union, the AUBTW in 1959. The men paid their subscriptions directly to me – as far as they were concerned, I *was* the union."

Charlie took redundancy in 1974.

"Steelworkers of today enjoy better pay and conditions of work than we ever did – but it has been at a cost. Where there were once 18,000 steelworkers in the town there are now only about 4,000."

He said the Anchor Works keeps the steel flag flying in Scunthorpe, but it would never have been built at Scunthorpe without the aid of public money.

He said better conditions on the steelworks would never have been achieved without the struggles and the sacrifices made by the fathers and the grandfathers of the present day steelworkers. Nobody should ever forget that.

Ashby High Street with the old pump at the junction with Bottesford Road.

Royal Review

A Coronation party under way in Newland Drive, Scunthorpe, in 1953. Many Scunthorpe and district communities marked the crowning of the current Queen in this way.

A really big moment for Angela Cooke came when she presented the Queen with a bouquet at the end of the royal walkabout on her visit to Appleby-Frodingham steelworks on May 7, 1974. Pictured with the Queen is David Joy, managing director of Scunthorpe steelworks.

Eat, drink and be merry… The Denby Close, Scunthorpe, Jubilee Party, held in June, 1977.

The King and Queen toured Scunthorpe steelworks in 1940. The King wore his Field Marshal's uniform, the Queen a powder-blue dress. Although details were not made public until that morning, crowds lined the streets. At the steelworks the King and Queen were accompanied by Lord Trent, Sir Angus Fillan, United Steel combine chairman Sir Walter Benton Jones, managing director C.J.Walsh, and W.B.Baxter, director and general manager of the company's plant in the Scunthorpe area. The processes at the plant were explained to the King and Queen by Albert Jackson, melting shop manager.

Pamela Teanby, Ealand's Jubilee Queen, rides past a house complete with Union Jack bunting and the numbers 25, signalling celebrations for Queen Elizabeth II's Silver Jubilee in June, 1977.

Northern Lincolnshire celebrated the Queen's Silver Jubilee in many ways during June, 1977. These ladies from Sherburn Crescent, Scunthorpe, donned patriotic hats and aprons – and got busy in the kitchen to produce special anniversary cakes for their street party.

Her Majesty the Queen at Barton in 1981 when she performed the official opening of the Humber Bridge, linking the two banks of the river.

Wartime

Gunness Auxiliary Fire Service members on an exercise during World War Two. From left: Tom Johnson, Walt Harrison, Walt Booth, Len Alvey, Herbert Spindley, Charlie Johnson.

Nylons were in very short supply during World War Two, and those who managed to obtain a supply were very keen to show them off. Some North Lincs women who could not get nylons resorted to using gravy browning to colour their legs and applied the seam with an eye-brow pencil!

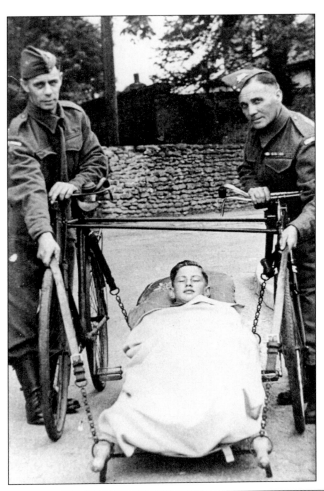

Alkborough Home Guard members Jack Bulleyment, Gordon Wynne and Fred Cousins with this bicycle ambulance. It was apparently the idea of Dr Ralph Baker of Winterton who was commissioned medical officer with the rank of captain.

Elsham Wolds was one of North Lincolnshire's main bomber bases but to keep every plane and its crew in the air required teams of hard-working tradesmen, including these ground crew members working on their Lancaster in 1943/44. Night after night the bombers set off from airfields like this in Lincolnshire and filled the air with a deafening roar as they headed out over the North Sea to carry out raids deep into enemy territory.

During World War Two, from 1939 to 1945, thousands of North Lincolnshire men and women were called to arms against Germany, Italy and Japan, and those who weren't did their bit on the home front. During the hostilities, Scunthorpe suffered remarkably little at the expense of the Luftwaffe, given its vital role as a steel producer. Gas mask drills like this one were carried out in Scunthorpe High Street but, thankfully, the life-saving devices never had to be used for real.

Brigg Home Guard members from the 1939-45 conflict. Although gentle fun was poked at *Dad's Army* in the hit TV series, the work done by the old stagers and teenagers who formed Britain's last line of defence was very important, certainly around 1940 when the threat of invasion by Hitler's forces was very real indeed.

Red Cross nurses on parade in Barton during Salute the Soldier Week, 1944.

Residents of Victoria Road, Ashby, marked peace with a fine Victory in Europe Day Party in 1945.

Personal Memories

Cecil Brumpton recalls cashing in those clothing coupons

PROUD communities have seen their local services almost fade away with the arrival of the motor car.

Cecil Brumpton pictured in 1998.

Cecil Brumpton, who was born in Kirton-in-Lindsey in 1928 and still lives in the town recalls swift rail journeys from London.

"When I was in the Navy I could catch a train from King's Cross at 3.45pm and get off at 7.40pm at Kirton."

While courting his wife he was able to catch a bus back from Hemswell at 10pm but rural services these days are somewhat limited.

"Kirton used to have its own Post Office and mail from here had a stamp, Kirton-in-Lindsey. The mail used to come here to be sorted. It left Manchester and arrived here at 4.15pm in the morning. On that train was mail for Scunthorpe to be off-loaded at Brigg to be taken by vans to Scunthorpe.

"All the services we enjoyed have gone. It makes a lot of difference to people wishing to get about."

He said that in his younger days Kirton High Street was full of shops and had two or three shoe outlets and numerous bakeries.

"I can remember horse-drawn vehicles fetching coal from the railway station to take it to farms for threshing."

He recalled also that water was taken from the pump in the Market Square and that water drawn from Ash Well was piped by Brigg Rural District Council to new council homes in Jubilee Crescent. Kirton also had its own gas works in Cornwall Street.

Cecil, of Ings Lane, was born in Town Hall Passage, Kirton, later moving to Barnard's Square (now demolished), East Cross Street and Jubilee Crescent.

His father Joe worked on farms and for Lindsey County Council. His mother Ruth worked on the land in gangs of ladies under Harry Clark.

Cecil attended the old Infants School in Wesley Street, the boys' school on the village green, the Junior school in St Andrew's Street

Kirton women working on the land with Cecil Brumpton's mother Ruth to the fore on the left.

He has been prominent in the Scout movement after joining the Kirton company in 1942 and serving as Scout leader, Scunthorpe and District Commissioner, and International Adviser for the County of Humberside.

and Huntcliff School which he left aged 14 to work at Perry's cement works in Gainsthorpe Road.

After Navy service he worked at Appleby-Frodingham as a blacksmith's striker but moved to work for Grant and Lyon in Scotter Road, Scunthorpe, and then Eagre's in East Common Lane. He has also worked for the Tidy Britain Group.

Cecil has been a Kirton Parish Councillor for 46 years, served on Brigg Rural District Council and was also on Glanford Borough Council.

Cecil recalled that in the early days the Scouts wore the traditional khaki shorts and big hats. He said people surrendered clothing coupons to obtain their uniforms.

He recalls proudly that until recent years Kirton was the seat of the district coroner and notes that Lady Godiva had been the first lady of the manor of Kirton through marriage.

The first air base in Kirton was established at Staniwells in 1918 but the main World War Two airfield which was home to Hurricanes, Spitfires and Defiants was on the site of today's Rapier Army barracks.

Kirton potato pickers with Cecil Brumpton's father Joe in the flat cap, centre right of the rear row.

Windmills

A super view of Wrawby post mill when it was still going strong in the early 1900s. Built sometime in the second half of the 18th century, it became the property of the Elwes family until the 1900s when it was bought by Mr H.Andrew, a member of a well-known local milling family who had worked it under the Elwes since 1885. He continued to work the mill until 1940 when it lost two sails and was subsequently abandoned. However, renovation began by a hard-working restoration group in the 1960s and the sails turned once again. It is now open to the public on a number of days a year, courtesy of the preservation society. From the top of Wrawby mill, standing on a prominent position on the escarpment of the Wolds, it is sometimes possible to see Lincoln Cathedral – 25 miles away.

Captain Jeremy Elwes (centre), of Elsham, was vice-president of the Wrawby Windmill Preservation Society in September, 1965 when the sails of the historic structure turned for the first time in a quarter of a century after costly reconstruction. The mill was completely rebuilt from the foundations upwards, and the beams provided by the president of the society, the Earl of Yarborough. Capt Elwes recalled that, 80 years previously, Lincolnshire could boast 250 windmills.

Bratley's flour mill was at Scawby Road, Scawby Brook – not far from where the mini-roundabout now stands on the A18. And here on Scawby Road we see some of the mill's finest being delivered in the firm's cart, although the mill itself is hidden by the trees. The driver is either William Smith (head horseman in the early years of this century) or mill owner Mr Bratley. The mill closed around 1932 and was dismantled.

The demolition of Garthorpe mill. This was the fate of scores of Lincolnshire windmills – no longer economic in times of developing technology. Some structures – the lucky ones – were transformed into spacious homes or pubs and restaurants.

Long Mill, Scunthorpe, was built by Uriah Long on the site of a post mill previously owned by William Wigglesworth. The brick-built windmill was in operation until 1920 and today forms part of the Old Mill public house.

Milson's Mill on Ferriby Road, Barton, was demolished in June, 1934 and its bricks re-used on the pair of semi-detached houses that now stand on the mill site. It was a six-storied tower mill which had been raised one storey since being built. Between 1872 and 1922 it belonged to George Milson, from whom the mill's name comes.

Ashby post mill stood at Ashby Turn and the last miller to operate there was Mr R.A.Ashbee. The top end of today's Ashby High Street was formerly Mill Road. A millstone from this structure was used to cover a well opposite St Paul's Road, Ashby, and was unearthed during demolition work in 1963.

The Isle of Axholme could once boast more than 20 working mills before they went out of fashion. But this imposing structure at Burnham is still standing.

A very familiar Brigg area landmark, Castlethorpe Mill, in the 1970s, before it was turned into the successful Artie's Mill restaurant complex.

Barton's Kingsgarth Mill was, for many years in the town's recent past, a blot on the townscape. Last worked around 1950 its condition deteriorated and in 1985 a local inquiry refused an application to demolish the building. Renovated and converted in 1991 as a public house and restaurant, the front of the building remains largely unaltered from its working days. The present mill was built on the site of an earlier smock mill which was probably destroyed by fire in 1760. Kingsgarth mill was also known as Kirkby's and Day's.

Fires & Disasters

Yarborough Mills – one of the best-known landmarks in the Brigg area – towards the end of a terrible blaze in 1910. Fire-fighting methods were found wanting, despite the gallant efforts of those on the barge. The blaze was discovered by a policeman and soon spread to the new part of the mills, where huge amounts of linseed cake and seed were stored. In 1989 history repeated itself when another blaze ravaged the then disused structure. It was subsequently demolished and the site cleared for housing development.

A fire at Bennet's cycle and toy shop on the corner of Frodingham Road, and West Street, Scunthorpe, in December 1969. The man at the bottom of the wheeled fire escape is thought to be fireman Pete Fillingham. It was the first time the Scunthorpe brigade had used its hydraulic platform. The blaze was about a week before Christmas and firemen Eddie Barrett recalled seeing disappointed children gloomily attending the scene. The man in charge was divisional officer Arthur 'Johnny' Johnson.

A famous fire at the Centenary Methodist Church, Scunthorpe, built in 1908 and destroyed on August 21, 1970. The alarm was raised at 3.25am and the ferocity of the blaze was such that by 4am the steeple on the top of the tower crashed into Frodingham Road. An *Evening Telegraph* report at the time noted: 'Soon the whole church was an inferno lighting up the sky, windows shattered and red-hot slates cascaded into the street.' The church hall beyond the left of the photograph was saved and a new church built on the site of the old one.

The charred interior of the Centenary Methodist Church after the fire.

The horrendous Nypro disaster at Flixborough on June 1, 1974, as captured by Evening Telegraph photographer Norman Reeder. There's no doubt that this was the biggest news story to happen in the Scunthorpe area this century. A terrible explosion ripped through the Nypro chemical plant, claiming 28 lives, injuring many and damaging property for miles around. Emergency services dashed to the scene and one of the biggest fire-fighting operations ever mounted in peacetime got under way. Norman was the first photographer on the scene and his pictures remain among the most dramatic ever taken of an industrial disaster. That Saturday afternoon had started happily with families enjoying the Appleby-Frodingham steelworks gala in Scunthorpe but, by 5pm, had turned into a nightmare.

Massive clouds of choking smoke rise from the huge blaze at the Nypro plant.

Every available fire tender from the counties surrounding Humberside was summoned to Flixborough to help in the battle to tackle the blaze.

Firms & Factories

Elswick Hopper marketed its products very well with brochures and publicity material. Doubtless this picture sold many of these cycles to local ladies. Now we see why they have always had the dropped crossbar – a throwback to the days when long skirts were a must for the genteel touring cyclist of 'the fairer sex'. Cycles were sent around the world courtesy of the skills of these workers from Elswick and Hopper Cycle Works, Barton. The firm was based in Marsh Lane with offices on the corner of Market Place and a foreign department on Brigg Road. Much of the production went to India and China.

Comedian Roundy Foster is pictured leaning out of the cab of a Progressive Bus Company bus around 1925. Roundy's stage name was 'Gormless, the Farmer's Boy'. His nickname, Roundy, came from his job as a motor mechanic and driver in the 1920s and 1930s when the town's bus firms included the Blue and the Red Progressive companies and Enterprise and Silver Dawn. Roundy was responsible for 'trueing up' the brake drums when worn. He would put them on a large lathe and roundy them up. His jokes were based on ridicule of officialdom with Ministry of Agriculture inspectors going on to farms ending up in pig muck or being chased by a bull. Roundy made various radio broadcasts and was also known for his knowledge of Lincolnshire dialect.

Hand diggers and metal wagon at Belton Brickworks, probably in the 1930s. Clearly hard, manual labour on a hot day like this.

Construction of items for the PLUTO project, Pipe Line Under The Ocean, used for the Mulberry Harbours in the 1944 Normandy Landings and built by Orthostyle at Ashby Ville, Scunthorpe. They wound a pipe-line round a drum-like cotton on a reel; they towed it on a large bobbin; laid it under the channel and across the Continent. They then pumped 1,000,000 gallons of petrol to our armies every day. Each bobbin, and there were six in all, was known as HMS Conun. Without these bobbins the job could not have been done. They were designed and constructed by Orthostyle.

Inspecting the bottling of milk at Clover Dairies in Scunthorpe.

Jack Cash, *Scunthorpe Evening Telegraph* linotype operator, seen on one of the machines at Telegraph House. All newspaper 'copy' used to be set in hot metal on these wonderful contraptions – a highly-skilled job. Today it's all computerised.

Snow, Floods, Storms

North Lincolnshire was already facing the threat of a German invasion in the winter of 1940 when things got even worse – a prolonged cold spell arrived and even the River Trent froze, as we can see from this striking shot of a barge marooned by the ice at Flixborough Wharf.

Travellers young and old wait by their stranded vehicles outside Bonby during the harsh winter of 1947. Grim days, indeed, for North Lincolnshire folk and particularly those living in the villages and hamlets.

A car tries to battle its way ever so steadily along the road to Sawcliffe Hill, near Scunthorpe, in 1947. The conditions bring to mind the words of the carol about snow laying deep and crisp and even.

The winter of 1947 was infamous for its severity and the hardship of North Lincolnshire folk was made worse by post-war austerity and rationing. Sawcliffe Hill, always seems to suffer most and was the scene of monumental snow drifts which had to be cleared by this mechanical excavator.

Powering through the snow on the Low Villages road, was this bus, believed to have started its journey in New Holland and heading for Lincoln, via Brigg. Many, during the winter of 1947, failed to complete their journey.

As pretty as a picture. This 1960s view of snow-sprinkled Bonby church would not be out of place on any Christmas card.

When it snows, photographers look for picture postcard scenes. And the old Briggate Lodge, near Broughton, made an ideal subject in the 1970s. The original Lodge was replaced by a Glanford Borough Council structure, before the site, in private hands, was transformed into what is now a marvellous hotel and golfing complex.

Although today's North Lincolnshire youngsters don't see a great deal of snow, when there is a useful fall they get out and about with their sledges, just as boys and girls have done for generations. Each town or village seems to have its favourite 'Cresta Run' and Brigg's is the slope leading into the Davy Memorial Playing Field, near the level crossing. In 1978 there was a prolonged spell of severe weather – and didn't these Brigg lads just love it!

Snow clearing under way at Humberside Airport, Kirmington, in February, 1978 – a vital task to keep the facility operational. From the look of the threatening clouds, more snow was on the way.

These Brigg youngsters demonstrate a novel way to save on the cost of shop-bought ice lollies – find yourself an icicle or two! The picture was taken in the late 1970s.

Few people alive today will recall when High Street, Scunthorpe, was hit by a tremendous downpour on June 22, 1909. The photo was taken just beyond Woolworth and the junction is the High Street, Wells Street, Cole Street crossroads. The sign above a shop on the left reads: 'Scunthorpe Steam Laundry Receiving Office'. The laundry was run by a Mr Gaundry. The Laundry itself was in Doncaster Road, Scunthorpe, which in those days was known as Clayfield Road. Beyond the junction to the left, set back, was the Trinity Methodist Church which was demolished in 1960 and replaced by today's BhS store. On the right there is a veranda walkway and what appears to be a wet fish shop. The premises on the corner are those of Bees the outfitters which shortly afterwards would be hit by fire.

Alan Barker, printing and stationery manager at Scunthorpe Civic Centre, answers the telephone in his flooded office in July, 1973. Torrential rain had fallen the previous night with the Scunthorpe Parks Department reporting 2.96 inches. Parks and playing fields looked like vast lakes and many steelworkers arrived home from the night shift to find floodwater pouring into their houses. The basement of the Civic Centre was flooded and serious damage caused to the printing department.

PC Terry Willis helps May Shipley to sweep floodwater from her home in Rowland Road, Scunthorpe, on July 16, 1973. The *Evening Telegraph* reminded its readers of the old wives tale that it will rain for the next 40 days if it rains on July 15!

WH Smith staff sweeping away floodwater from their store in Scunthorpe after a huge deluge in July, 1973.

This youngster makes the most of a huge downpour in Scunthorpe in July, 1973 – with a boat trip on the flooded Kingsway Gardens.

Youngsters in Scunthorpe in July, 1973 didn't need computer games to keep themselves amused. These lads are taking full advantage of flooding in Kingsway Gardens for a cooling paddle. Who needs Cleethorpes beach?

There was severe flooding along the banks of the River Ancholme in early May, 1981 and this was the scene on what should have been the first day of the cricket season at the Brigg Sugar Factory ground, Scawby Brook. An official inquiry was held at the Angel Hotel, Brigg, when angry farmers slammed the Anglian Water Authority for its handling of the situation. But an AWA official said three inches of rain had fallen in 69 hours – almost double the average for the whole month. Although the pumping and drainage equipment worked efficiently the sheer magnitude of the rainfall was overwhelming.

Agriculture

The Scunthorpe district has long been a great growing area for potatoes – now picked by machine and moved around by tractor and trailer. Back at the turn of the century, however, it was a case of hand picking, depositing into a horse-drawn wagon and storing in the fields – protected by layers of straw to keep out the frost – before moving them away to market.

Alice and Annie Driver with cows at the back of their house in Carr Lane, Appleby.

Jack Baines ploughing at Hibaldstow *c.*1920s.

Many hands make light work on Mr Clark's farm at Thealby in this 1950s view of harvest time.

Harvesting under way at Gunness in August, 1957 with Normanby Park steelworks away in the distance.

Elsham station in the background as harvesting is carried out in the 1950s.

A scene once familiar on every Lincolnshire farm but now mere history – old-fashioned haystacks at the end of a hectic summer. This view was taken in Winterton during the 1950s.

A horse is led through the centre of Scawby in the late 1950s as a tractor passes by with a load of wood, probably from the nearby Nelthorpe Estate.

A fine collection of cabbages being harvested by a team of ladies in this field in the Brigg area during the early 1960s. Note the little girl in the centre of picture who had to accompany mum to work.

The centuries-old practice of using horses to power farm machinery was almost at an end in North Lincolnshire when this picture was taken in March, 1963. The ploughman is clearly a veteran of many years of honest toil on this stone-strewn Lincs farm.

Cows passing through North Kelsey for milking in the 1960s.

Potato picking by hand was back-breaking work but offered very useful money for many a North Lincolnshire housewife looking to budget ahead for Christmas. Here we see workers picking the few remaining 'tates' in a field for Burwell Farming Ltd at Elsham in the late 1960s.

The *Whirlybirds* TV series would have been all the rage on television at the time when this helicopter pilot earned his corn spraying fields in the Brigg area.

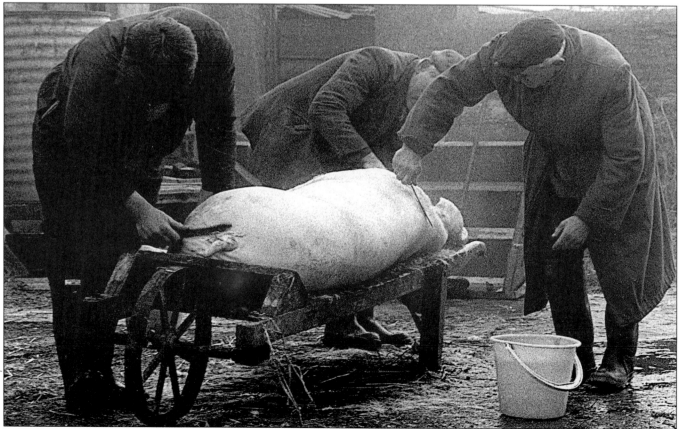

This was the annual scene in many rural North Lincolnshire households – the pig that had been fattened during the year was killed, and then the carcase cleaned. Later the animal would be butchered and the meat preserved for use over the months ahead. This picture was taken at Hibaldstow.

Well-known Wrawby farmers Richard, Jack, Colin and Robert Day pictured at Tong's Farm in March, 1966.

A delightful view of a prize pig relaxing in his North Lincolnshire sty during the 1960s. His pose seems to suggest a very happy life.

A van belonging to the well-known North Lincolnshire firm of Peacock and Binnington out in the fields offering assistance in this Brigg area view from the late 1960s.

Hedges are now a less common feature than they were in the British landscape, with the move towards bigger and more cost-effective fields. But the job of keeping hedgerows in good repair was once an important one on many a North Lincolnshire farm, as we see here.

Personal Memories

George Curtis recalls a farmworker's life

LIFE on the land in Lincolnshire was hard in the 1930s but there was a sense of community and skills aplenty among the workforce.

Some families lived in tied cottages, though many were almost itinerants moving from one job to another.

George Curtis, of Broughton, born at Tattershall in 1925, lived in a number of rural communities including Croxton, Willoughton and Corringham.

He worked on the land from his childhood days through to 1959 when he became a full-time employee of the National Union of Agricultural and Allied Workers.

George was based in Brigg as District Organiser from 1961, dealing with the interest of rural workers in an area stretching from Lincoln to the Humber.

He has a deep understanding of life on the land and says that while many farmworkers were called labourers they had more skills than many who looked down their noses at them.

"There were skills associated with working horses and the implements associated with them.

George Curtis.

"To get a good day's work out of the horses you have to understand the animal and it has to be properly fed. It has to be yoked to an implement.

"The needs of the horse was paramount. If the horse had a sore shoulder it could not work."

George said that, before the war, the bulk of heavy work on farms was done by horses.

"The first tractors I saw were in the 1930s. They started doing the heavy work, ploughing and cultivating land. The horses still did the drilling (putting the seeds in)."

After the war, tractors were more numerous, but the loss of workers from the land was gradual with many leaving for higher wages at the steelworks and others going due to increased mechanisation on the land.

Another of the skills that has passed by with the arrival of Dutch barns is stack building.

This involved packing the straw into loaf-shaped masses so as to channel water away and protect it from strong winds.

George said the skills in tying sheaves and loading them on to a lorry were not often appreciated.

Ploughing and building potato graves (in which potatoes were protected by straw and soil) were also skills to be mastered.

He said most of the farms on the Wolds were mixed – with sheep, cattle and horses – and self-sufficient on energy.

Food was grown for the animals which worked the land, unlike today when land is devoted to cash crops.

Farm workers grew food in their cottage gardens and kept pigs and hens.

"When I was young I worked hard but I lived well. You did rabbiting which would supplement the beef and bacon.

"There was a sense of community. You

George Curtis and his sister Joyce astride a motorcycle at the family home at Cliff Farm, Willoughton, around 1936.

could trust people. They were honest. If you left anything about you knew no one would run off with your bike or coat."

George is a member of North Lincolnshire Council and previously served on the Lindsey and Humberside County Councils.

George Curtis of Estate Avenue, Broughton, with a tractor.

Medical Matters

Scunthorpe's Cottage Hospital at the junction of Cliff Street and Rowland Road was established in 1886. In 1892 it suffered a setback when the premises failed to meet the requirements of the sanitary authority. A new hospital was mooted but in 1899 it was extended with the addition of a 12-bed ward and an operating theatre. In 1929 the 30-bed hospital was replaced by Scunthorpe War Memorial Hospital.

Scunthorpe War Memorial Hospital replaced the Frodingham Cottage Hospital and was dedicated to those who gave their lives in World War One. The foundation stone for the hospital was laid by Lord Buckland of Bwlch, on October 13, 1927 and it was opened by Talbot Cliff JP on December 2, 1929. The cost of building, furnishing and equipping the Hospital was £65,000. The hospital with 72 beds was built in 14.5 acres of land provided by Lord St Oswald of Nostell Priory whose family also had Appleby Hall.

The new nurses' home at Scunthorpe War Memorial Hospital which was opened by HRH Prince George on October 26, 1933. The foundation stone was laid in October, 1932 by W.Benton Jones. The Nurses' Home contained 58 bedrooms for nurses and in addition to the usual offices, also included lecture, demonstration, study and sitting rooms and a kitchen for the teaching of the principles of sick-room cookery.

The opening of Scunthorpe Maternity Home in Brumby Wood Lane, Scunthorpe, in 1936 by Sir Kingsley Wood. The hospital was demolished and replaced by a housing estate in the late 1990s. From the left: Connie Spavin, unknown, Edith Polwin, Akehurst, unknown, Matron Hill, unknown, Sister Hancock, Connie Garton, Edna Fowler.

Sport

Ashby Mill Road FC of 1920-21 – clearly a successful season with a handsome cup and two shields to display. Note the trainer with the towel draped over his shoulder – a practice still common in boxing but lost to soccer.

Trophy-winning Santon Athletic Football Club during the 1922-23 season. There is still a Santon team playing today in the Scunthorpe League.

Later to become a professional footballer with Grimsby Town and manager of England, Graham Taylor (third from left, front row) began in the school team at Henderson Avenue, Scunthorpe, in the mid-1950s. In the year above him was future golf professional Tony Jacklin.

Scunthorpe United (white shirts) in action in the FA Cup first round, against non-League Skelmersdale at a snow-bound Old Show Ground in 1967. On the left of the picture is the superb cantilever stand built in the late 1950s with Scunthorpe steel. United won 2-0 with goals from John Colquhoun and Frank Barton (penalty). The Iron lost 1-0 in the second round at Halifax.

Ray Clemence – later to find fame and fortune with Liverpool, Spurs and England – features in this Scunthorpe United team picture for 1966-67. Back row: manager Freddie Goodwin, trainer Jack Brownsword, Keith Burkinshaw (later manager of Tottenham), Geoff Sidebottom, Ray Clemence, Frank Burrows, Frank Barton, John Barker, Barry Horstead, Barrie Thomas, unknown. Middle row: John Colquhoun, Pete Neale, Bobby Smith, Derek Hemstead, Micky Ash, Dave Sloan (later a Northern Ireland international), Brian Bedford, Barry Lindsey. Front row: Stuart Bramley, unknown, unknown, unknown, Stewart Taylor. Ray was with the team between 1965 and 1966. He made 50 League and Cup appearances.

During his days as manager of Sheffield Wednesday, England World Cup hero and later Republic of Ireland soccer manager Jackie Charlton attended the annual dinner dance of Messingham Trinity FC held at the Berkeley Hotel, Scunthorpe, in April, 1978.

In March, 1984 former England and Liverpool football star Kevin Keegan returned to the town where he began his professional football career to open the new council-run leisure centre. He was with the Iron from 1968 to 1970 making 141 League and Cup appearances and scoring 21 goals. He lodged in King Edward Street. Kevin was appointed England manager on a temporary basis in February 1999.

A super bird's-eye view of the Old Show Ground – long-time home of Scunthorpe United. The ground was demolished in 1988 when the Iron moved to the outskirts of the town and a brand new purpose-build stadium, Glanford Park. The Old Show Ground site was then transformed into a Safeway supermarket.

Brigg Town Cricket Club's team, *c*.1908, which won the solid silver Dinsdale Trophy, later to be competed for by teams in the Broughton and District Evening League Knockout Cup. Brigg Town was a major club in the late 19th and early 20th centuries but folded in the early part of World War Two. However, the club was reformed in 1973, largely through the efforts of Brian Parker and Coun Bryan Robins, and has just celebrated its silver jubilee.

West Indies cricket legend Garry (later Sir Garry) Sobers seen while playing in the Appleby-Frodingham cricket festival of 1961. Sobers (third from right, front row) is with well-known Scunthorpe player and former Pakistani Eaglet Salim Uddin (extreme right, front row) and Festival sponsor Lt Cdr Gerry Wells (centre). The generosity of the steelworks management meant that many top names from the world of cricket came to Brumby Hall during the 1950s and 1960s for Festival Week, which usually included a visit by the Lincolnshire side for a Minor Counties fixture.

Later to be a professional cricketer with Worcestershire and coach to England A, Phil Neale, the young lad pictured on the front row (extreme right), was a member of this Appleby-Frodingham Cricket Club side which won the Lincolnshire League title in 1972. Phil was one of the last professional footballer-cricketers, turning out for Lincoln City and helping them to the Division Four title.

England cricket legend Ian Botham taking part in the floodlit cricket match at the Old Show Ground, Scunthorpe, in September, 1980 when Botham's XI defeated a Scunthorpe Select side. The match was organised by solicitor and keen local cricketer Michael Heath – now Judge Heath. Botham, who lived at Epworth, also played soccer on the ground making 14 League and Cup appearances for Scunthorpe United with additional outings in the reserves.

Olympic cyclist Albert 'Lal' White, from Scunthorpe, and members of his family while he displays the Muratti Cup to crowds of onlookers. Lal won 15 national championship titles and prizes to the value of £6,700 which included 55 Cups outright and 100 medals, including a silver at the Paris Olympics in 1924. He died in 1965.

Hockey sticks have undergone a radical change in appearance since this picture of Appleby-Frodingham Men was taken in the late 1940s.

Brigg Hockey Club's team which took part in the annual festival staged by the Appleby-Frodingham club at Brumby Hall in 1979. Still playing for the Brigg club are Adrian Broome (back row, third from left) and Peter Spittlehouse (centre, front).

Scunthorpe and District Table Tennis Association players pictured at Brumby Hall, Scunthorpe, in 1944. From left: Geoff Creasy, Bernard F. Goy who now lives in Bournemouth and used to run the Walburn Construction Company in Midland Road, Scunthorpe, and Raymond King of Doncaster Road, Scunthorpe. Bernard played for the Scunthorpe Table Tennis Association and Appleby Frodingham.

Double Open champion Tony Jacklin – the Scunthorpe area's most famous golfing star – seen at Brigg Recreation Ground in June, 1970, where he presented prizes at the Preparatory School sports day. The previous year, Tony had become Britain's hero when he landed the British Open title at Lytham St Annes, while in 1970 he followed that up by winning the United States Open.

Angling is Britain's most popular sporting pastime and the Scunthorpe area is well served with fisherman and clubs. In addition to the River Trent, the Ancholme is a popular venue, including the tranquil Cadney Road stretch in Brigg, seen here in the 1970s.

Winterton's Kevin Armitage (front) takes the inside line at Ashby Ville while racing for Scunthorpe Stags speedway team in a Monday night National League encounter with Middlesbrough Tigers. The other local rider in the picture is Ian Gibson. Speedway enjoyed mixed fortunes in Scunthorpe, the local team beginning as the Saints at Quibell Park and moving down to The Ville where there were ambitious plans for a super stadium which never came to pass, the team dropping out of the league in 1985.

Spectacular action from a stock car meeting at Ashby Ville, Scunthorpe. This sport drew large crowds to the local stadium on Saturday nights before the plug was pulled. The stadium was demolished to make way for the Lakeside retail development.

Members of the Scunthorpe Steelers American football team, which played home games at Quibell Park, seen in April, 1985. Gridiron might seem a very unlikely sport to gain a foothold thousands of miles from its traditional home on the other side of the Atlantic. But it caught on in a big way in Scunthorpe during the 1980s, the Steelers enjoying plenty of success. For a time the HQ of one of Britain's top leagues, the Combined Gridiron, was based in the town on the Queensway Industrial Estate.

Personal Memories

We played football with a future England manager, says Norman Reeder

CHILDHOOD sci-fi movies at Scunthorpe's Royal Cinema through to men on the Moon have been witnessed by retired *Evening Telegraph* photographer Norman Reeder who was behind the lens to capture local history for over 50 years.

He grew up in the long since demolished Old Row, Santon, with the old ironworks behind it and the Redbourn steelworks and a giant gasometer to the front.

"I still retain vague memories of an early childhood happily spent playing in the muck and grime and the constant jump into the old tin bath tub in front of the fire to get it off."

He also recalled the 'Twopenny Rush' at the Royal Cinema (now the Blarney Stone pub), where *Flash Gordon's trip to Mars* starring Buster Crabbe was the Saturday matinée serial not to be missed.

"Recollections move onto the important time spent during the war as blackout monitor at Henderson Avenue School, making sure no chink of light escaped to lead night-time raiders to our mighty steelworks which would be the Germans' prime target according to our headmaster, the all know-ledgeable Mr W.E. 'Rambo' Ramdsen."

The war disrupted education with lessons switched to homes, Norman attending classes at Mrs Button's in Highcliff Gardens.

"I also recall how proud the whole school felt many years later when hitting the headlines as former pupils Graham Taylor and Tony Jacklin were appointed bosses of England's football and Europe's Ryder Cup golf team

Norman (right) on the way to see *Flash Gordon* with brother Don pictured at Old Row, Santon.

Queen Elizabeth opening the model traffic area in Laneham Street, Scunthorpe in June, 1958.

respectively and a 1954 *Telegraph* photo of them in the school football team was resurrected and splashed all over the national sports pages.

"Graham was in at the birth of Sunday football in the town as an overworked left-half in Reeder's Rascals when still a grammar schoolboy, while Tony's early golfing talents were nurtured under the guidance of Ted Muscroft, the professional at Scunthorpe Golf Club."

Norman attended the 'Brown' school in Cole Street but was more interested in the angles on the tables at the YMCA in High Street (now part of the Living Store) than trigonometry and logarithms.

In days when jobs were plentiful, Norman, already a *Telegraph* newsboy delivering papers to the King Street, Princess Street and Sutton Street area (now the multi-storey flats) was

taken on full-time by *Evening Telegraph* office manager Eric Guitard in April, 1944.

"I graduated from being a darkroom printer in the mornings, Bush machine printer in the afternoons, and a 21 dozen and four newspaper boy at night, to become a fully fledged junior cameraman when photographer Harry (Sandy) Sanders was taken ill and I was pressed into service, despite never taking a picture in my life, with the big plate camera.

"The firm's carrier bike (no staff cars in those days) and I became inseparable."

With each day throwing up a diversity of assignments from royal visits to revelling in the mud with the 'Boggins' at Haxey Hood, Norman never thought of leaving the town. Fires, floods, explosions, crashes and murders plus diary engagements meant there was never a dull moment.

He recalled news editor Mick Robins who

Ted Muscroft next to the legendary Bobby Locke. Ted was the professional at Scunthorpe Golf Club in the 1950s when he coached Tony Jacklin who was later in charge of the Ryder Cup golf team.

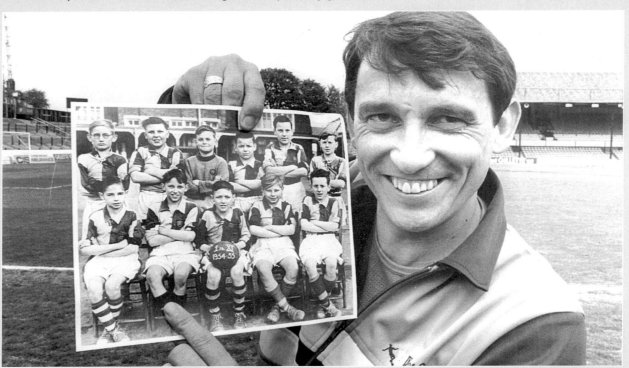

Graham Taylor who became England soccer manager points to himself (front row) and Tony Jacklin (back row). They were both members of the Scunthorpe Henderson Avenue soccer team in season 1954-55.

Queen Elizabeth opening the Scunthorpe General Hospital extension, The Queen's Building, on May 19, 1993. The £15 million project included multi-speciality wards, an ante-natal clinic, central delivery suite, a special care baby unit, five operating theatres, an anaesthetist services department and administrative areas.

was in control on the fateful Saturday of June 1, 1974 when the country's biggest peacetime explosion devastated the Nypro works at Flixborough. Norman was disappointed a special Sunday edition of the *Evening Telegraph* was never published but says regrets were few.

"As the only journalists on site before roads were sealed off we had my exclusive pictures and those taken at the hospital by

Norman on his retirement.

colleague Roy Archer, in addition to all the stories gathered in by reporters who had rushed in to cover the catastrophe and a readership wanting to know.

"As we entered the 1990s so the days of black and white photography and darkroom printing, like those of myself, were numbered.

"Colour and computerisation were fast taking over and retirement in April, 1995 seemed pre-ordained."

Norman was taken aback when Scunthorpe Borough Mayor Christine Pearson presented him with an inscribed borough plaque to mark his 50 years' service to the town and invited him and his wife Laura to join her and consort husband Jim on an official trip to a Buckingham Palace garden party.

The snapper snapped – Councillor Jim Pearson's shot of Norman and his wife Laura at the palace.

Pubs

The Friendship pub on the banks of the Stainforth to Keadby Canal in the early part of the 20th century when square-sailed keels took goods to industrial towns on the inland waterways network.

The Lion's Head in Park Street, Winterton, in 1905. The licensee was Thomas Capps Mabbott, a retired compositer who had been an overseer on the *Liverpool Gazette,* and Mrs Mabbott.

The George Hotel, Barton, around 1906. It was the venue for many important meetings relating to town affairs including the arrival of gas lighting. The George was also the main watering hole for those visiting Barton cattle market which continued to be held into the late 1950s.

An early view of the White Hart Hotel, Crowle, with carriages outside. More is the pity that buildings cannot recall the history which surrounds them. The oldest name recorded among past landlords is a Mrs Ann Cattle up to 1868. To 1872 a Thomas Peart held the licence for four years. William Dackles was landlord for the same term. The interior pub beams came from a ship wrecking yard at Gainsborough.

The Magna Charta Hotel in New Holland before 1910. The premises were named after one of the ferry boats. There were ferries from various communities across the Humber but New Holland gained prominence with the coming of the railways. For a brief period the village was on the main eastern rail route from London to Scotland, which ran from Bishopgate to Grimsby via Peterborough, then from Grimsby to New Holland, across the river to Hull, then by train to Selby and York for the north. Houses were built at New Holland for people working at the station and by 1850 warehouses, cattle sheds and coal wharves had been constructed. Work on the jetty installations was completed in 1851.

The Queen Hotel, Rowland Road, Frodingham, around 1910. The premises were opened on October 12, 1898. The hotel was commissioned by Thomas Woodruff Woodley whose family bottled beer. Thomas's son William Woodley subsequently ran the pub until the family vacated it on April 6, 1922. He was well known in town, affectionately called King Billy. He was a Justice of the Peace, a member of Lindsey County Council and the Frodingham and Scunthorpe Urban District Council. He was also a member of the Brigg Board of Guardians. Tom Woodley (William's son) is to the right of the doorway.

The Travellers Rest Inn, Burringham High Street, pre-1920. The landlord in the early part of the century was William Theaker. The pub no longer exists.

The Station Hotel, Scunthorpe dwarfed by scaffolding. It was built in 1888 and demolished in 1958. This picture was taken towards the end of its life.

Staff at the Station Hotel, Scunthorpe, around 1920. The building stood near the old railway station and was dwarfed by giant structures of the Frodingham Iron and Steelworks to its side.

The old Red Lion Pub, Kirton. The ladies seem happy to pose for the cameraman.

The Bay Horse Hotel, Garthorpe, in the 1930s. The pub is the last in the village with other hostelries the Plough Inn and Webb's Hotel by King's Ferry on the River Trent having closed. In early 1999 the Bay Horse itself had been closed for some months. Fox's prize ales were brewed in Crowle. The landlord in the 1930s was John Harrison. Petrol at one stage was sold from a pump at the front of the hotel.

The Unicorn Pub that was, Kirton-in-Lindsey.

With its abundance of foliage, nowhere was quite like the courtyard at The Angel Hotel in Brigg when it came to enjoying a pint or a bar meal. The Angel, historically linked with the old stage coaches which plied their trade in centuries gone by, sadly had to close as a hostelry. But, in recent years, North Lincolnshire Council has restored the market place landmark and turned it into offices. Brigg Town Council, meanwhile, operates the Angel Suite function room.

'A load of mischief' outside Scunthorpe's Blue Bell Hotel in 1935. The hotel in High Street was one of the town's leading establishments in the early part of the century with a horse-drawn omnibus link from the former Great Central Railway Station to the hotel. Its landlord was Robert Ingham Swaby who died in 1915 and was succeeded by his son Arthur. The hotel, which was close to the old bus station, was sold to Shipstone's Brewery and demolished in 1970 as part of the town centre redevelopment.

The Lord Nelson Hotel in Brigg was up for sale in 1968 when this picture was taken. But, despite changing hands several times, its frontage is still recognisable to drinkers of today.

The Blue Bell Hotel in High Street, Scunthorpe, not long before its demolition in 1970.

Brigg is said to have more pubs than any other town of comparable size in the north and is the only one to boast a hostelry called The Dying Gladiator, seen here around 1970. The sculpture of the gladiator takes pride of place above the entrance to the Bigby Street pub and was produced during the 19th century by the multi-talented William Clark who converted a house into the inn. One school of thought says the then landlord was inspired by Lord Byron's poem about the Dying Gladiator; others that it was modelled on a statue he saw on a visit to The Vatican.

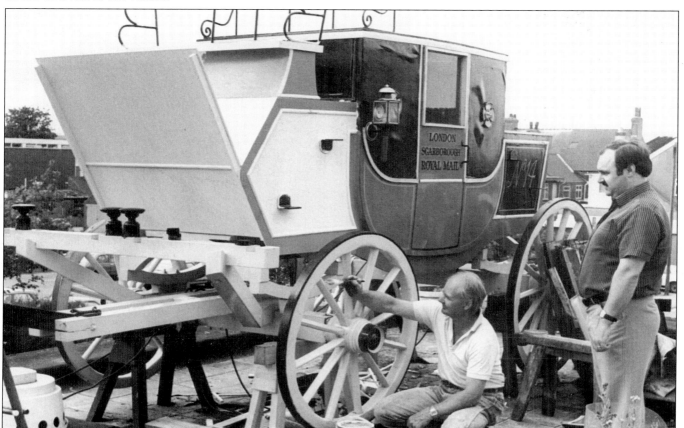

A London to Scarborough coach which was on the roof of the single storey extension at the back of the Parkinson's Arms Scunthorpe, in the 1980s with Malcolm Cain, the landlord at the time, on the right. The coach is no longer there.

Clubs

The Scunthorpe and District Workingmen's Club in Normanby Road, Scunthorpe, once had showers and baths in its basement. It was known locally as the Big Social and stretched back to before 1911. It is now a snooker hall and until recently housed JJ's disco.

One of the most popular groups to play Scunthorpe clubs from the 1960s onwards were Tony and the Cadillacs, fronted by local businessman Tony Borrill (second right) who has now settled for the sunnier climes of Magaluf, Majorca. Other group members pictured are Mel 'Fingers' Oliver (keyboards), Alan Harsley (lead guitar), Mick Cowling (drums) and Mal Evans (bass guitar).

Brumby Hall Social Club steward Derek Spavin offers pet dog Ace a pint of best in this 1970s view – long before the current drink 'Two Dogs' became popular. Which would Ace have preferred?

Representatives of ten Scunthorpe area clubs who reached the 1974 Clubland Queen finals. The winner was Jane Moore, second from left on the back row.

Janet Brown (centre) is crowned Miss Brigg Town Queen at The Hawthorns, home of Brigg Town Football Club, in August, 1977. With her are runners-up Susan Parker (left) and Angie Benson, while club president and Town Mayor, Coun Bryan Robins, adds his congratulations.

If the Pogson brothers – Wilf (left), Don and Bob – had to play their trump card in 1978 it would be the three of clubs. For the trio were chairmen of three different social venues in the Scunthorpe area. Bob was chairman and concert secretary at Brumby Hall Social Club, Wilf was chairman of the Burton Stather WMC and Don was chairman of Ashby Institute. All three worked for British Steel in Scunthorpe.

The winner of the 1978 Scunthorpe Clubland Queen contest, Polish Social Club's Jennifer Kralski (centre) with runners-up Karen Hill (left) of Winterton WMC and Pam Enefer, Miss Reform. The Reform is now the Mayfair.

Sheree Cox, from the Isle of Axholme, won the Scunthorpe Clubland Queen beauty contest in October, 1979. This event involved each of the many Scunthorpe area clubs holding its own heat, from which the qualifiers were judged at a grand final.

Steward and stewardess of the Cemetery Road Club, Scunthorpe, Ralph and Margaret Johnson, had good reason to smile in November, 1979 for their popular steelworkers' venue had just officially opened a big extension. Drinkers were offered specially low prices by way of celebration with beer at just 21 pence a pint. Among those appearing at a special concert was comedian Paul Shane, then travelling the northern clubs but later to find fame in TV comedy series like *Hi De Hi*, *Oh Dr Beeching* and *You Rang M'Lord*.

Steward Stan Davey gets among competitors in the Frodingham Road Club Easter bonnet parade. Left to right: Barbara Hame, Yvonne Taylor, Muriel Strutt, Winifred Jackson, Florrie Smith and Betty Johnson.

Riverside Reflections

The Aegir on the River Trent towards Gainsborough. The Aegir is believed to have originated with the Vikings in whose legends the Aegir was a giant who was lord of the seas. Aegir had a wife called Ran (ravisher). It was her who stirred up the waves causing them to lash violently together imperilling the ships upon the jaws of the Aegir. The level of the water rises until the weight of the heavier sea water gains supremacy and again flows upstream. It is when this flow reaches the long stretches of shallow water that it breaks into menacing waves. The largest bores are in spring and autumn.

The Aegir, or bore, on the River Trent has claimed the lives of a number of North Lincolnshire people down the years, mainly through dangerous attempts to ride the waves. And here we see a couple of men in the early part of the century risking their own safety in a flimsy rowing boat.

A whale beached in the River Trent off Meredyke, Garthorpe, in 1901. A number of whales and seals have been spotted up the river over the years.

Vessels on the Trent at Keadby pre-1914. The original Keadby Bridge is just visible in the background with the old fertiliser works with chimney on the right. The new lift bridge was built between 1914 and 1916.

People on a steamer on the River Trent approaching the original railway-only swing bridge, opened in 1864 and subsequently replaced a few yards downstream in 1916 by the current Keadby King George V road and rail bridge. Steam packets sailed from Gainsborough through to Hull on a regular basis, calling at various riverside villages en route.

The Steam Ship *Harrogate* (1,029 gross tonnage) was built in 1925 and was typical of many of the vessels which sailed along the Humber and up the Ouse to Goole carrying goods a plenty. Both the railway companies and Co-op operated fleets of similar steam vessels from Goole.

The Norwegian Steam Ship *Neptun J. Laurentzen* in the 1930s ran on to Whitton Sands with a full cargo of coal. All the crew were saved. The sands claimed many vessels. As the tide fell they often broke their backs. Few ever got off the sands. There was a local jingle: 'Between Trent Falls and Whitton Ness, many are made widow and fatherless.'

The typical interior of a cabin on a sloop. The one pictured is the inside of the *Amy Howson* owned by the Humber Keel and Sloop Preservation Society. Prior to World War Two families could be found along the Trent and Humber living in such conditions in sloops and keels.

Crowle Wharf, 1930, looking towards Godnow Bridge.

Yachts in the 1930 Regatta at Owston Ferry.

Sculling on the River Trent at the Owston Ferry Regatta of 1939. The regatta drew crowds of 5,000 as both villagers and those from other riverside communities competed in sporting activities including swimming races, blindfold sculling, sailing and plucking a flag from the the end of a greasy pole jutting out from a tug on the river. The last regatta was held on August 7, 1939, though villagers staged a revival event on July 19, 1986. Regattas were staged by communities along the Trent and Humber.

The King's Ferry landing stage at Garthorpe in the 1940s looking towards Burton Stather shortly before the ferry ceased to operate. In the early part of the century Webb's Hotel was open by the jetty to provide accommodation on the busy route from the West Riding of Yorkshire into Lincolnshire. The building of a road link across the River Trent at Keadby in 1916 took away most of the traffic.

Barges on the frozen River Trent. The river froze in the bad winters of 1940 and 1947 but nowadays it is argued that power stations upstream pump warm water into the river, reducing the likelihood of such freezing. Scores of people have given accounts of how they actually walked across the river.

The Maltings at Barton Haven during demolition in 1971. They malted barley used in the making of wines and beers. During World War One the Maltkilns were used for drying wheat and barley salvaged from ships sunk by U-boats with the grain then turned into cattle food.

Village Views

The Sun and Anchor public house features in this old picture of Scotter. The hostelry continues to enjoy good trade in the village to this day.

The Market Cross, Epworth. The lamp has long since gone.

Westfield Road, Goxhill, around 1906 with Dale's Shop at the far end, now Eastfield House.

Wrawby Church looks much the same today as it did seven or eight decades ago when the photographer perched his tripod on what is now the A18 to take this charming view. Given the volume of traffic passing through the village today we would be hard pressed to repeat his handiwork.

George Johnson's coal wagon making deliveries at North Kelsey, with George and his brother Arthur. The boy in white is Cliff Johnson. The vehicle is a Bedford two-tonner and was used for delivering coal around North Kelsey in the 1930s.

A super scene of rural life in Cadney in the 1950s, machines being belt-driven from the tractor.

A picture postcard view of Appleby during the 1950s, featuring a local mum and her young family (centre).

The landlord of The Bay Horse at Garthorpe sweeps up outside his premises as (left) a young girl takes her labrador for a walk. The long shadow thrown by the telegraph pole would seem to suggest high summer.

Broughton in the early 1960s with the rickety shop (left) looking sadly neglected, unlike the parish church.

The market place, Barrow-on-Humber, in the days before motor cars became popular, and when quiet leafy lanes were to be found, even in the centre of North Lincolnshire villages.

A super panoramic picture looking out over the village of Barrow-on-Humber some 30 years ago.

A lazy summer day in Amcotts with villagers, out for a walk, passing the church in the mid-1970s.

The Magna Charta Hotel in New Holland. The wall has now been demolished and the road to the left is no longer a through road.

Out & About

Barton has a long tradition of cycle manufacture and sales, but this two-seater machine is a far cry from the BMX and mountain bikes of today. Still it was a great way for a man and wife, or fiancé and fiancée, to get out and about in the fresh air – together.

Attending Winterton Show in 1903 was a great excuse to get dressed up in your Sunday best, whether you were a toff or a tot. And donkey rides were an optional extra!

Showing dogs at the Scunthorpe Show in July, 1909. Which did the judges choose? The spectators seem to be making their minds up.

Scunthorpe's Old Showground, on the site of today's Safeway store, has been the site of many a community activity. The trimmings on this car and costumes worn by the occupants suggest they are taking part in some kind of carnival but there are no markings on the picture suggesting what it was.

The Spavin family roller skaters, who were world champions, at the Pavilion Roller Skating Rink which was in Doncaster Road, Scunthorpe, and which later became a cinema. Back: Dave, Ralph, Jack, Fred, Septimus, Olman. Middle: Jessie. Front: Joseph, father William, mother Mary Jane and Harry. The family had lived in Frodingham but moved to Digby Street, Crosby.

Amcotts championship tug of war team in the late 1920s. The team members were farm workers, bar the trainer holding the cup who was Amcott's headmaster Mr Shoebridge. From left, back: Jim Ellas, Jim Brown, William Sylvester, Alf Johnson, Jim Ellas snr, Alf Prescott. Front: Ted Hewitt, Mr Shoebridge, Tommy Harrison.

The Locke family outside the cottage in Carr Lane, Appleby where they lived. Their father George Locke was the butler at Appleby Hall. He had previously been at Nostell Priory.

George Locke who was butler at Appleby Hall which was destroyed by fire on March 15, 1933. He was butler there for around 33 years and died in the late 1920s.

In the 1920s and 1930s the Co-op was the most prominent retailer in Scunthorpe and North Lincolnshire with branches in many villages. A carnival was held at the Co-op fields in Brumby Wood Lane each year with individual villages entering floats for the carnival parade. The Winteringham float featured here encouraged people to drink 'Grade A' Co-op milk.

Members of the Strength and Fitness Club's ladies' section which met in premises behind Todd's shop in Oswald Road, Scunthorpe, during the 1930s. Featured, from the left, are: Violet Franklyn, Cissie Leake, Ena Cross, four unknown, Phyllis Targett (née Freeborn).

Ron Davis and his wife Rita on their 1936 BSA 350cc motorcycle in front of the cottage behind Walcot Hall where they spent their honeymoon in 1939.

Members of the Messingham Church Council laying the footpath from the church gates and leading up to the church entrance. The photograph was taken about 1939/40. The people from left are, Cyril Cheesman, unknown, Tom Brown, Revd Hollborow, Harry Cheesman, unknown, Mr Richardson and Grant Marshall.

Pupils at a Christmas nativity at Crosby School around 1942. Centre group (top): Joan Bunn. Top middle: Brenda Lowe and Irene Featherstone. Bottom middle: Edna Mahon and Sylvia Campsell. Left back: Tony Senior, unknown, Glen Jackson, Roland Jones. Front left: Brian Theaker, unknown, and Pat Cropper with child. Right back: Michael Overton, Ivor Davey. Front: Norman Grant and Ivor Sanderson.

A floral display in Kingsway Gardens, Scunthorpe, in 1957 marked the 21st anniversary of the inauguration of the town as a borough.

Carol Hesslegrave (left) and Jennifer Vamplew (later Caldow) on their bikes. Forty years ago there was far less traffic than there is today but the town elders of Scunthorpe deemed a model traffic area should be built, and these young ladies gained full marks in their cycle training.

Retained firemen Graham Emerson and Andrew Liess on Hemswell ejector seat training with the fire brigade, about March, 1958. It was training to get people out of ejector seats. At that stage Hemswell was still a fully functional airbase. Afterwards firemen were provided with special knives for cutting the harnesses that held the airmen in.

Glamorous staff of British Home Stores, Scunthorpe, in 1962, including long-serving Ann Brumpton (second left) who went on to become manager.

Central Park paddling pool, Scunthorpe, offering marvellous, free entertainment to generations of Scunthorpe youngsters on those hot summer days.

Spectators watching with interest at Winterton Show in July, 1964. This event has stood the test of time and is still going strong today.

Taking a well-earned rest, having attended to some maintenance work at the turf maze called Julian's Bower, Alkborough, are Raymond Barnard (left) and Herbert Gaunt. An explanatory plaque provided by Sir John Dudding, whose family own the maze, was built and erected on site by Herbert Gaunt in the summer of 1976. The exact use of the maze is unknown. It is mentioned by the curate of Broughton Abraham de la Pryme in 1697 who referred to it as a Roman game (Gillian's Bore). He also noted there was a maze at Appleby. The maze pattern set into the floor of Alkborough Church porch dates from 1887.

Horses being shown in the ring at the Winterton Show in 1964. Both the braces-wearing attendant and the horse seem happy to look the cameraman's way.

Early 1970s shoppers wait patiently for the arrival of a Lincolnshire Road Car double-decker at the bus station – an area of the town centre now earmarked for redevelopment. The bus station, opened in February, 1969 by the Mayor of Scunthorpe Coun Alice Cropper, replaced an earlier one run by Enterprise and Silver Dawn in Scunthorpe High Street next to the Blue Bell Hotel. The first bus into the station was driven by Sam Budworth.

Children with their mugs at the Appleby-Frodingham steelworks gala held at the Brumby Hall sportsground in 1978.

The days of the Lysaght's gala were almost numbered when this shot was taken at the July, 1981 event. The traditional gala mug, being sucked by the toddler, proudly proclaims this to be the 57th Normanby Park gala. When the steelworks closed it was a severe blow to the Scunthorpe economy.

Central Park – central to Scunthorpe's proud boast of being an industrial garden town. Acres of well-tended greenery in Queen's Gardens and Central Park offer a quiet place to relax.

East Butterwick around the turn of the century.

A Penny Farthing race at Normanby Park Show, 1908.

High Street, Barton, before motor cars made posing for the cameraman a hazardous occupation.

Pupils at Winterton Church of England School in the 1930s.

Employees of Layne's, the Brigg motor dealers, pose with a fleet of delivery vehicles belonging to Prescott's, the well-known North Lincolnshire dairy firm, in the 1950s. Billy Harris and Charles Taylor are on the extreme left.

Normanby Park lido which was where the Victorian Garden is now.

Contestants in Scunthorpe Borough Council's family weekend beauty contest in 1980.

A raft race at Ealand in September 1981, with old brickwork chimneys in the background.